Catch Me if I Fall

Dear Pauline

with love & gratitude

Nikki

x

How Mental Health Broke My Back but Didn't Break Me

Nikki Rodwell

Copyright Page

Published by **Nixie Books**

Cover design by **Cutting Edge Studio**

Copyright © 2021 by **Nikki Rodwell**

Catch Me If I Fall

ISBN: 978-1-9163989-1-7

Thank you for purchasing my book.
Visit this link for your free gift of My Photo Journey and
to sign up for my newsletter.
https://nikkirodwell.co.uk/book-readers/
(link also at the back of this book)

Dedication

This book is dedicated to my husband for his unconditional love and support and showing me that love really does conquer all.

To my dad who sadly passed away in March 2021 before this book was published and who will be sadly missed.

MIRROR MIRROR
ON THE WALL,
I'LL ALWAYS GET UP
AFTER A FALL,
AND WHETHER I RUN,
WALK OR HAVE TO CRAWL,
I'LL SET MY GOALS
AND ACHIEVE THEM ALL.

Contents

Chapter 1

The Bubble Is Burst

On 19 July, 2019, I was rushed to A&E at the Norfolk and Norwich General Hospital on a spinal board. I was alive. I have only hazy fragments of memory, since a bit like childbirth, the brain excels at erasing the intensity of such pain to protect the mind. But then what protects the mind from itself? How do you erase the dark nightmares of something so horrific that I don't fully comprehend to this day that it really happened to me and wonder if maybe I am writing about someone else?

The journey in the ambulance was a ride of terror. I believed I was in a hearse. The last breath of air was sucked out as the paramedics bolted the doors, leaving me trapped in this vacuum with muted sound, where a scream wouldn't be heard even if I attempted one. I felt the vehicle pull away, my mind frozen with terror, believing I was being taken to a local crematorium where my family, daughters and friends would be waiting to watch as I was ceremoniously brought out strapped on this board, for a fate worse than death. A brief flash went through my mind which showed a bird's-eye view of the paramedics carrying me towards the chapel with my head turned away for fear that they would all see my shame. They were all shaking their heads in disappointment, crying with pity, knowing what fate I had coming— that I was to be burnt alive in front of their very eyes. I was paralysed with fear; it all made sense to me now… a slow, humiliating death was what I had coming to me. I felt I had done something bad that deserved punishment.

My terror rendered me catatonic, small judders of breath catching in my throat and my face frozen. As I lay there silently, with my eyes tightly shut, I braced myself for an eternity of torture which I had no way to avoid.

Once we arrived at A&E, I was confused. Why hadn't I been burnt alive? Where was I and what the hell was happening? It was all changing so fast, like flicking through TV channels in an erratic and crazed manner. Imagine for a moment falling asleep on a train that you believed to be taking you to the bright lights of the city, only to wake up as you pull into a seaside resort at the end of the line, jolting you into a confused state of reality. Well, that is exactly how it felt; I had landed at a different destination but there was still a sense of some ominous persecution coming my way.

My head was locked in place with an immobiliser brace, and I caught a brief glimpse of bright lights above me before being wheeled into the artificial light of a building with faces looking down at me and voices that kept repeating my name. *'Nicola, can you hear me? Nicola?'* I was dazed; there were voices and bright lights in all directions. It was chaotic and loud on the outside but inside it was strangely quiet. I just glared, wide-eyed, trying to process something, anything. I was trapped in my own horror story and needed to work out where this was going next.

Once inside, there were medical staff rushing in all directions and the sounds of heart monitors bleeping and I believed I was in some kind of drama that was being orchestrated around me. My paranoia kept me guarded; I couldn't let them know that I knew. My body remained in survival mode, all my senses ready for fight or flight (although I wouldn't be going anywhere strapped from head to toe to a board).

There was a reason I was surviving this. *Someone* was playing a game with me of some sort, *someone* was out to "get me". There wasn't a single soul left on earth I could trust, least of all this clinical army of people buzzing around me. There was no one to help… I was caught in a loop of unending fear where all things horrific were possible, an infinity of nightmares playing out before me, with no sight of a calm or happy ending.

I was prodded and poked and asked lots of questions, feeling like an animal in a laboratory. As the nurses cut off my clothing, I truly believed that I had been abducted by aliens and was now in their spaceship about to be analysed. The aliens were cleverly disguised as clinicians, the most convincing-looking doctors and nurses I'd ever seen. They kept asking me to move certain parts of my body, which I did, too scared not to cooperate. The only part of me I couldn't move was my legs. I think my toes may have moved a little, but my legs weren't moving at all, and I wasn't sure whether it was me doing this or whether it was part of the game.

A doctor came and introduced himself with a few colleagues who began touching me with little pins up and down my body, asking if I could feel them. I would just nod or shake my head, playing along with their little game. My speech was monosyllabic, and perhaps they all thought this was due to shock, since nobody had told them yet that I was in the middle of a psychotic episode.

It wasn't long before my poor husband Martin arrived and rushed to my side. I feel more than terrible today that I put him through all this, especially the way that I spoke to him from this point. But in my mind, I couldn't trust him either. This wonderful, loving man who is the other half of my heart, was my enemy, and in fact, I suddenly realised he was the evil "director" of this unfolding show that I was in. He had always had a love of amateur theatre and his real passion lay in directing; of course, it was all coming together now.

Film after film played out before my eyes. Everything I saw, heard and felt, triggered a flashback of one film or another. I remember seeing the large metal air conditioning ducts suspended from the ceiling and believing I was in the film *Aliens*. There was no Sigourney Weaver to help save me though, and I felt helpless as I anticipated the A&E nurses pulling out machine guns at any second to shoot any escaping aliens. It sounds far-fetched, I know, but believe me, I would have been less scared with the true reality unfolding; that I was in a holding bay in A&E with my head in a brace strapped to a spinal board with the prospect of a life-changing injury.

In the midst of the toing and froing of medical staff, I recall having a vivid flashback of Martin biting his nails and shaking his head in disbelief whilst talking to doctors. At the time I believed this indicated his disappointment in me, shaking his head like a frustrated teacher whose only option was to put a naughty child into detention again.

Strangely, there are snippets of memories I can recall with great clarity, but other chunks have just dissolved away, like a sandcastle being taken by the tide. Thankfully I don't recall any great physical pain during this stage, but then again I was attached to a morphine drip, and perhaps my detachment from reality also detached me from any pain; the mental pain being greater at this point in time.

They soon wheeled me off for the first of many scans. I recall jumping into an episode of *Star Trek* when I was taken into radiology. I held my breath whilst being fed through the CT scanner, believing it was going to hurt me in some way. Despite this sounding somewhat humorous, in a "Beam me up, Scotty way", it was actually terrifying. I had no clue as to why I was actually there or what they were looking for. No, in my world, I was like a child on a journey of discovery, being taken through a playground of terrifying scenes, with nobody to hold my hand.

Once I was wheeled back to the holding bay, the doctors broke the news to Martin. I had fractured my T12 vertebra, quite spectacularly as it happens. The lower thoracic vertebra had what's known as a "burst" fracture and had been smashed into pieces with some fragments of bone pressing on my spinal cord. This was to become the most complicated part of my injury; the SCI (spinal cord injury) was what was concerning the doctors the most.

The prognosis was grim. Poor Martin, who is renowned for coping in a crisis, was tested to his limit that day with the devastating news that there was a strong possibility that his wife would be doubly incontinent and never be able to walk again. Our perfect little world, our Norfolk bubble, had just been burst.

So, it would seem that I'm an "all or nothing" kind of girl at times. Do a job well, or don't do it at all. This even seems to be the case having escaped breaking a single bone in my body up to the ripe old age of fifty-two, and then spectacularly breaking my back whilst in the grip of a psychotic episode. Another thing in true "all or nothing" style; I have no low level chronic mental health condition but then experience an out of the blue, acute psychotic episode.

But before I tell you more about this, perhaps you should get to know me a little before we continue with my bizarre story. Let me tell you about me and my perfect little world that was about to be shattered.

I'm just an ordinary, middle-aged woman, heading towards the dreaded menopause. I seem to have what they call the menopausal "brain fog" which has similarities with baby brain and, invariably, if I lose something, it's either in the fridge or on top of my head!

I never stand still for long, always on the lookout for a new challenge or opportunity. I am naturally inquisitive and a soul-searching individual who has learnt much from life's lessons over the years, including the ability to change. Not in a "chameleon changing colour" kind of way, but rather becoming a better and more successful version of myself. I am competitive and very driven, a bit of a perfectionist perhaps, always seeking to become the best version of myself that I can. My husband would say that I need structure in my life to function well and that whatever I turn my hand to, I do well. He is my biggest supporter.

I live in a little village in North Norfolk near the sea, with Martin and two dogs, Chester and Mabel. Imagine a picture postcard cottage with roses around the front door, in a secluded country lane in a peaceful, rural location, surrounded by fields and trees, with the sea visible in the distance... Well, that's where I live, in a beautiful, quiet spot of the North Norfolk countryside, settled in a quaint little village with flint cottages that wind around a twisty little road with a church and a... church. Yep, that's it! No shop, no pub, nothing else. Well, unless you count a village hall with a green.

It took quite some persuading to move me out to such a remote spot, believe me. As we pulled up on the gravel driveway, my arms were firmly folded and my reluctance clear at being brought out to "just come and take a look". But the double-fronted cottage with roses around the door and its perfectly sized front garden, was beckoning me to come in and just take a look!

It was surprisingly bigger inside than it had looked from the outside. I feigned interest in a wood burner that caught my eye in the kitchen, plus there was an open fireplace in the lounge. I had never yearned for an open fire, what about the dust? Well, we all have to make compromises, so on seeing the three large double bedrooms, one for my office, one for my daughter Chloe, and best of all the huge main bedroom with stunning views stretching across the adjoining fields, I was persuaded.

The only thing apart from its rural location that deterred me was the expanse of side garden, which almost felt like it didn't belong to the house. It could be seen over the waist-level flint stone wall from the front garden in which there was a small gate from which to gain access. But it felt like it belonged to next door, as if it was divorced from the rest of the house and I said as much to Martin when I first clapped eyes on it.

'Nope, it all belongs to this cottage, and besides, I need a new hobby. I've always wanted a big garden to look after and grow my own vegetables.' Big was an understatement. I felt the front garden was plenty big enough for us and our dogs, this garden seemed overindulgent, excessive. My look of disbelief must have been apparent to Martin, who tried to reassure me.

'We'll be like that couple from the TV series we watched when we were younger.'

'You mean *The Good Life*?' I laughed. 'Well, I have been likened to Felicity Kendall in my younger days.'

The Good Life was a seventies sitcom in which a young couple in the suburbs tried to be self—sufficient, their efforts constantly hampered by their snobby neighbours, Margo and Jerry. Felicity Kendall played the very attractive young woman. Penelope Keith was Margo, the snobby neighbour…

'More like Margo…' said Martin.

Now there most certainly is no comparison here, since I am no snob, although there may have been times when I've sounded a tad like her. For example, on our first trip to a garden centre, I did get bored rather quickly, and asked Martin indignantly, 'Can't we get a man in to do this?' Well, it was boring, and I hate gardening — aisles of perennials and bedding plants really aren't my thing! I'd far rather be in a Next store looking at clothes or choosing things for the home.

So, we decided the house was a perfect fit. We would become the new tenants and make it our home. It was a little nerve-wracking for me since this was the first time I was to rent. I had been a homeowner since my early twenties, but we had quite a few debts to clear and I wanted to be free of that burden. Martin convinced me that the location would work well, after all, most of his decorating work was in the area, which would mean far less travelling for him and, since I mainly worked from home, it did seem only fair. The truth be known, I think he also wanted to move back to living near the sea. He once told me how he feels at one with himself when walking on the beach, especially with our dogs.

It turns out the expanse of side garden is a good thing since both of our dogs love its excessiveness, taking full advantage of the large lawn down the end where there is an array of pear trees, apple trees, and beautiful greenery — I haven't the foggiest idea what it's called— I am not green-fingered in the slightest! I do however know the name of the Pampas Grass as we have a particularly large one that Mabel, our bouncy black Labrador, circles around in a crazed manner when she has an attack of the zoomies, usually with something in her mouth that she shouldn't have, and taunting Chester to chase her. Chester is our black and white Springer Spaniel who is older, pushing ten now, and not amused by the puppy antics of his sister Mabel!

Martin is husband number three, but as the saying goes — third time lucky and ain't that the truth! He is larger-than-life, both in stature and personality, with a passion for acting and singing. He takes life as it comes and is very much a "live in the moment" type of person. He is the yang to my yin: he has his head in the clouds and is the dreamer in our relationship; I am the realist who keeps us on the straight and narrow with feet firmly on terra firma. He would say that love makes the world go around whilst I believe money is also needed, especially for quality of life and to give us choices. He also says "possessions are your leg irons", but I have visions of a nice home, holidays and a comfortable retirement.

But life is about learning, and the biggest lesson Martin has taught me is to love, like I have never loved before. Not just him, but also myself; it's like feeling the sun both inside and out. His love for me is an unconditional, all-encompassing love which gives me the safety to truly explore myself, to be me. He loves taking care of others and I often say how everyone needs a "Martin" in their life. Especially when having a crisis…

I think any man would have been devastated to receive the news that their wife may be confined to a wheelchair, paralysed from the waist down, but poor Martin not only had to process this information, but also break the news to his psychotic wife. The woman who was ordinarily his best friend was a complete stranger to him right now.

I was lost … still "on set" in my delusional world. This, coupled with being high on morphine, meant I didn't process the severity of the situation at all. Probably a good thing. I have a very vague memory of Martin leaning over me, desperation in his eyes.

'Nikki, do you hear what they're saying? You may never walk again!'

All I focused on was his desperation, misinterpreting it for anger and hostility, so I became hostile back.

'Well, you've got what you always wanted; you can have it all now. The perfect "ending" for your little show. The café, all my money, I'm stripped of everything. My father was right when he said if I moved to Norfolk, I would end up alone and impoverished!'

Wow, I think perhaps I really *had* been taken over by aliens.

I find it hard to comprehend the complete shock it must have been for Martin in the midst of this drama, to receive this news. That something had just happened which would throw our lives upside down forever and perhaps leave his wife disabled in a wheelchair from this day forward. I don't suppose he had ever imagined when we got married on a silver white beach in Cocobay Resort, Antigua, that he would be faced with something quite like this. "In sickness and in health." Truer words have never been spoken. He must have felt so alone.

But then again, so did I, single-handedly fighting my battle against the universe, trying to survive. I could not have been further away from Martin had I been on a beach on the other side of the world. Strangely though, during some vaguely lucid moments, I did have a flicker of awareness that there would be no going back from this. My unconscious was trying to nudge me back to reality every now and then by hinting that I was going to be put in a psychiatric hospital, seemingly aware at times that I was in psychosis.

Mr Lomjay, the spinal surgeon, whom I remember so clearly to this day, came and explained to me the details of the operation that I needed to fix my vertebra. It was a process called "spinal fusion" which involved putting metal screws and rods into the vertebrae above and below the fracture to stabilise my spine and give the T12 a chance to heal. He would also try to remove the fragments of bone pressing on the spinal cord, but any damage caused would be irreversible since nerves do not regenerate. This operation would give me the best chance of being able to walk again, although it was by no means guaranteed.

He may as well have been speaking in a foreign language, since I processed nothing, apart from the word "operation", telling myself that I didn't want one as I recalled my grandfather had never fully recovered after an anaesthetic when he was in his later years. Then, Mr Lomjay added to my confusion by giving me an alternative. The other option was to let things "heal naturally" without operating, which meant my recovery would be a much longer process with an extended hospital stay. This also had an uncertain outcome but could quite possibly be worse.

'Leave to heal naturally?' Yes, that sounded so much better! Why have an operation if nature could do the job? My brain was analysing the information with the mentality of a primary school infant, as if I'd been asked if I'd like to climb a tree or go on the swings.

The surgeons were all on their starting blocks ready to go ahead with the operation there and then, but I refused. Poor Martin was about to learn that you can't reason with a "crazy" person and he did everything in his power to try to get me to change my mind. As he leant over me, desperately begging, his tears fell on my face. I ignored his pleas and turned my face to the side, crying out for some more drugs as I could feel pain starting now. Somewhere deep in my back, a horrible gnarling sensation was emerging. I closed my eyes and refused to look at him, or anyone. Why were they all making such a fuss? I just wanted to be left alone. I wanted to feel safe again.

Chapter 2

My Knight in Shining Armour

Now I have no idea whether it was a few hours or an entire day that I spent in the A&E department since there was no concept of time in my world. I was suspended in some twilight zone which had no beginning and no end, no night and no day. I was taken up in a lift and wheeled onto a ward somewhere on the fourth floor in the central block of the hospital. I have no recollection of arriving there.

Martin was left to take up the gauntlet with the nursing staff. How could his wife, in the midst of psychosis, possibly know if she needed an operation right now? He virtually clambered over the nurses' station to try to speak to the sister on duty, imploring her to help him. They simply had to go ahead with the operation, he knew it, and he knew they knew it too.

Martin was mid-flow with the confused sister when she told him that the surgeon was already in a meeting discussing my dilemma. Her eyes briefly glanced towards a door on which a notice read, "Meeting in Progress", and, like some kind of superhero, Martin burst into the room which was full of doctors, nurses and surgeons.

'How dare you have a discussion about my wife without me being here.' Even the chair flinched as he planted himself down to direct the meeting.

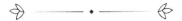

Martin the actor. Confident, larger than life, a little boisterous and can occasionally come across as a tad "arrogant" to some people. Not me though. It made me laugh the first time he used his phrase 'Do you know who I am?' in a pretentious act of self-superiority. That's what it is… an act. Yes, he is confident, not scared to be a little outspoken at times, to wear luminous pink socks or a shirt and jacket that make an outrageous statement, to step in with his size elevens and tell someone when they are behaving like an "arse" when they're belittling their wife in a shopping queue. No, he doesn't live ruled by fear of judgement from others like many people do. And that's a life skill that has slowly rubbed off on me and given me a confidence I never knew I had.

I was still slightly battered and bruised by my pre-Norfolk days when we first met back in 2009, lacking in confidence, living a life restricted by the boundaries of social phobia and fear of what others thought of me. I used to hide behind his rather large physique (he says he has broad shoulders) when we were socialising at one of his after-show parties or committee luncheons (my worst nightmare). But he would hold my hand tight and help integrate me with his friends and, dare I say, "fans" in the amateur theatre world. I was soon to become his biggest fan though, after seeing him play the lead role in *The Crucible* and, by contrast, Edna in the musical *Hairspray*. My pride and admiration for him grew beyond measure.

'They all love you,' he would say to me, trying to convince me that I was wrong in my belief that his friends didn't like me and trying to get me involved, which I eventually did. I even ended up treading the boards on more than one occasion, playing the role of "Widow Corney" in a production of *Oliver* in front of a scary 450 spectators on Cromer Pier. Yes, he brought me out of my shell bit by bit, and the new Nikki began to flourish… It wasn't long before I would be on the other side of the room to him at parties, his tell-tale wink at me signalling how proud he was, knowing that I now felt comfortable holding court on my own, chatting to people openly and honestly. This man discovered the true me who had always been trying to escape, and with it I blossomed into a confident, bubbly, and life-loving woman. We were a perfect match.

Now Martin isn't exactly the "Prince Charming" in the looks department that I had in mind in my younger days, in fact, I used to joke that he was my "Shrek" which backfires nowadays since he calls me "Donkay!" I kissed a lot of frogs on dating sites over the years before finding him and the truth is (and he does know this) I wasn't physically attracted to him when we first met. But that's okay! I loved his confidence and his charismatic personality, and he was quite unlike anyone I had met before, secure and strong in himself with an infectious zest for life and kind beyond words.

I think it would be fair to say that I fell in love with his voice first, his deep, comforting tone that would not be out of place on the radio or presenting a TV show. Then his larger-than-life personality won me over. Yep, this man is large in everything but especially when it comes to love. Despite being an only child, he has learnt to be totally selfless, undemanding of his own needs, whilst he loves others unconditionally; something I'd never experienced before. He will go out of his way to give of himself in time, love and energy, which is especially true with my two youngest daughters who were still at home when we first met. It was Chloe and Steph who persuaded me to stick with him when I had doubts, and I'm so glad that I did. It taught me another lesson in life: that you can fall in love with someone *after* you get to know them. It doesn't have to be that careless "can't keep your hands of each other" type of love, wooed by the initial wave of lust, but rather getting to know the true person and forming a deep friendship *before* having the physical connection and then discovering true love can follow. Well, it worked perfectly well for me anyway. This man was to become my rock, my soulmate, my everything. He loved this imperfect girl perfectly, even when she got a little crazy.

So, time was running out, and poor Martin was fighting to save his wife the best he could, to give her the best chance of walking again, to pick up the threads of life that she had left behind. It was a Friday, for God's sake, and if decisions weren't made now, they would probably be held off until Monday!

There was a fair amount of confusion going on in the meeting since the surgeons had never come across this situation before. But with Martin's boot firmly up their behinds, they all agreed to immediately refer the situation to the legal department of the NHS, requesting that they section me as a matter of urgency to render my decision to avoid the operation null and void.

Thankfully this is exactly what happened; I was sectioned under the Mental Health Act, solely for the operation to take place. Oh, what a fuss I caused, and I'm embarrassed to this day that this all had to happen. Apparently, it was the first time in thirty years of being a spinal surgeon that Mr Lomjay had had to section a patient before carrying out an operation. I certainly think I left a lasting impression!

Now, had I been more agreeable, the operation would already have taken place, but as it turned out, once I had been sectioned, there was a major emergency in the hospital. There had been a horrific road traffic accident meaning the operating theatres were unavailable and my operation was delayed for two days. This meant I had two very dark nights to get through.

Being on a ward with lights flashing, buzzers ringing and a whole host of other strange new noises, whilst in a psychotic frenzy, is pretty awful. With my senses all heightened, it became a cacophony of confusing sounds. I remember being petrified that some sort of werewolf-type creatures were going to come in and tear us all apart in the night. I saw shadows creeping across the ward, from under the other beds. I heard the staff saying out loud the thoughts that were in my head. There were strange sounds coming from the dark corners of the ward. I believed with every bone in my body (apart from T12) that this was all leading to a very slow and painful death. I almost yearned for this now; death would surely get me out of this misery.

But the next minute my mind would switch and tell me that I was already dead, and this was my hell that I could never escape. The dark horrors I was experiencing were exhausting. Every second felt like a minute, felt like an hour, felt like a lifetime.

At some point in the night, there was wailing from another room. I would later learn that it was a long-stay patient with dementia, however, in my madness, I thought it was someone being mauled to death by some gothic beast, half-human, half-animal. My mind conjured up a horrific bloody scene just out of view. I was going to be next, torn to shreds with no one to save me. I had to escape.

I tried to pull myself up, not knowing I had a broken back and was supposed to remain perfectly still. I managed to move my knees a little and was able to push up onto the backs of my arms but exhausted myself as I tried to grip the sides of the bed. A nurse saw me and rushed to lay me back down, telling me off for trying to move. Oh God, I was trapped here. Some practical joker had frozen my legs; they weren't working! I couldn't run now even if I tried. I was powerless, at the mercy of whatever was coming for me. I shut my eyes and prayed. My body did not allow me to sleep all night; the panic kept the adrenaline pumping through my veins.

As dawn broke and light began to seep onto the ward, I began to sense a new apocalyptic event was about to emerge, and it was all going to be my fault. My course of actions, my very being here right now, meant that there was going to be some massive global catastrophe bringing about the end of civilization!

I nervously started turning all of the rings on my fingers. Gollum from *The Hobbit* springs to mind. It's a good job I can make light of this, otherwise I might cry as I tell you that I actually believed one of those rings could make me invisible.

Oh, the rings… during my madness, they had all been systematically switched from finger-to-finger numerous times until I had got them all just right. Many things had been obsessively fixated on during the psychotic delusions, including jewellery; I spent hours in my bedroom going through the contents of my jewellery box, changing rings and bracelets around because suddenly certain things had superstitious significance. I believed if I didn't follow the signs being given to me, something terrible would happen either to me or, worse still, to someone I loved. Gold was evil, silver was good. 'Oh God, that ring was given to me by my daughter.' It had to be worn on a certain finger to keep her safe. It sounds ludicrous, but one by one each ring kept being moved or changed because of some complicated thought process happening in my head.

I now had the task of keeping them safely in place on their chosen fingers as I believed they had some power to keep me and, in fact, the world, safe. I twisted one ring 180 degrees on my finger, believing at that moment that it would prevent the apocalypse from happening, for now anyway. This is why I reacted so badly to being told I needed to remove all my rings for an MRI scan before the operation, because the metal upsets the scanner. I became distressed and agitated, belligerently telling everyone that I was not going, and they couldn't make me. Martin tried to reassure me that I wouldn't be alone, that it would all be okay, and there was no need to be scared. I think he believed I was fearful of the MRI scan itself as I had never had one before. Well, he was half right, since I also believed that should they succeed in getting my rings off, this film was going to change course again. I had another vision of being buried alive, this time by being slotted from my hospital bed into a tomb encased in a wall. They would trick me that it was an MRI scanner when in fact they would place me into a crypt and seal it up with stone and leave me there to rot. I can see now that this delusion must have come from a memory of seeing my Spanish stepsister being buried when I was just nineteen. Her coffin was slotted into a wall in a Spanish cemetery, which was more like a massive filing cabinet for the dead. It's the way things are done in Spain.

A nurse reassured me that I could keep my wedding ring on throughout the scan, but I was terrified to take the others off, so it was no consolation. Neither was being told that they would all be kept safely locked up in a little safety box on the wall by my bed for when I got back.

I panicked as I became aware of the nurses gathering to collect me for the scan and after turning my "Gollum" ring to make myself invisible, I slipped one of the other rings off my finger and swallowed it! Yep, I actually swallowed a ring, and without water too. But there was another ring that I needed to keep with me as a matter of life and death. It was an adjustable ring that could be pulled apart, enabling me to slide on a little diamante gem from my Pandora bracelet, which I believed represented the planet. I popped this into my mouth, right at the moment a nurse swept in through my curtain.

'Nicola, what's that in your mouth?' It would seem I wasn't invisible after all!

I was like a naughty child refusing to open my mouth and spit out the contents. She immediately called for help and nurses came rushing in all directions. It was now or never, I had to do it. There was no logical thought process warning me that I could possibly choke, no fear that it could get stuck in my digestive system or cause me some harm. I just had to swallow it, get it into my stomach for safe keeping.

As I gulped it down everyone was suddenly yelling at me, asking what I had just swallowed, so I told them. They were making so much fuss! And then they were talking about me, like the bullies in a playground; they glanced in my direction whilst whispering under their breath, but I could hear them…

'Did you see that? The lunatic has just swallowed her rings! Like she thinks that is going to save her…' The reality was, of course, they were concerned for my wellbeing, asking each other if anyone had seen exactly what I had put in my mouth; how many rings had I actually swallowed?

Martin arrived at my bedside and calmly stroked my face. I think he was crying. I just turned and looked the other way. He was my enemy right now; he was in on the plan to destroy me, to do away with me. Life had tricked me.

I successfully avoided the MRI scan, and thankfully it wasn't long after that the mental health team came to assess me. They put me on quetiapine, which is an anti-psychotic drug, with immediate effect. Thank God! I was started on a low dose of 25mg which would also turn out to be the maximum dose I would need.

Somewhere in my mad world, I became aware that I was waiting for an operation which I knew I couldn't escape. I felt like a helpless fly caught in a web, just waiting for my painful end to come. I was nil by mouth until after the operation, but as I kept asking for water, I felt I was being tortured with everyone deliberately depriving me of this basic human requirement. I was hand-fed little sponges on a stick that were soaked in water for me to suck from time to time. I remember wondering if people had done this for Jesus Christ on his journey to Calvary, perhaps remnants of my Jesus delusion. I whined like a petulant child, demanding a proper drink of water, but none came.

The following morning, after another exhausting night of battling demons and other horrific scenes in my head, it was finally time to be wheeled off to the operating theatre.

Yet another film played out in my mind a film – a film from my childhood called *A Matter of Life or Death* in which an RAF bomber pilot (played by David Niven) from World War II escapes death when his plane crashes. It depicts his journey falling in love and ending up on an operating table fighting for his life, looking down on himself from above as they remove his brain tumour. During this life and death operation, a scene plays out where he has to argue for his right to continue his life having cheated death. He fights his case in front of a celestial judge and jury and ultimately wins, which allows him to be returned to his body and survive the operation. I truly believed this was about to happen to me and I remember desperately sending a text to my daughter Chloe as they wheeled me out of the ward, saying that if I didn't survive the operation, she simply had to watch this film and then she would understand! I didn't believe I would win over the celestial jury and would not make it through.

It felt like I was on death row now as they wheeled me silently down endless corridors, ceiling panels and bright lights flashing past me. I remained silent, but in the odd flicker of lucidness, I just looked at Martin, fearful and pleading for an end to this nightmare. He was there the whole time, holding my hand.

I started crying, yet another fear coming over me. I now believed with utter conviction that I was going to be awake on the operating table. It was going to be one of those freak mishaps you read about, where the anaesthetic only works partially, with the patient still conscious but paralysed and unable to communicate. The terrors just kept on coming, almost like a psychotic form of Tourette's, but instead of inappropriate speech bursting out, the worse possible nightmares were bursting into my mind. All the while I felt that somehow, I deserved to be punished and now the crescendo was going to reach its climax.

Ironically the first attempt at putting the anaesthetic into my hand didn't work and despite counting up to ten, I didn't go under. This didn't help the panic going on in my head at the time! As the anaesthetist tried for the second time, I could hardly breathe and looked at Martin with fear in my eyes. Thankfully, oblivion came.

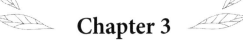

Chapter 3

Change Is Good

I moved to Norfolk in 2007 shortly after I turned forty, in search of a peaceful life. I needed a fresh start after nearly a decade of awful events including a horrific divorce, relationship let-downs, family fallouts, misplaced loyalties and a whole host of dramas. It was a dramatic step to take, but a necessary one. I had blindfolded myself and played "pin the tail on the map" which landed on Norfolk, a county I knew very little about other than it had no hills and was subject to interbreeding, according to its many non-supporters. It was wildly out of my comfort zone since I had never been very independent and was painfully lacking in confidence, but thankfully, against all odds, I made it.

It was tough being a single mother of two in a new county and I didn't adapt very quickly to my new life, not in the early days anyway. I missed my eldest daughter Amy, as did her sisters. She had remained behind in Surrey to continue her A-Levels after matters had been taken out of my hands (like so many) by a family who didn't agree with my move. Despite difficulties in family relations, I had always encouraged my daughters to maintain healthy relationships with their grandparents which seemed to backfire on me in the end. Torn between a family and her father surreptitiously undermining me by offering to support her to stay or moving to Norfolk with me and her sisters with the upheaval of a new school, she chose to stay. This, amongst other factors, led me to start drinking, feeling isolated and wallowing in loneliness. I had no one in the world to turn to, not even family, and I remember calling Samaritans at my lowest point – a desperate call at three o'clock in the morning, snot streaming down my face, wine glass in hand, as I blubbed down the phone telling a complete stranger how hopeless life was, that I was all alone, and I didn't know how to carry on. I was so lost, fumbling around in a grey fog of despair. They say life begins at forty and yet here I was making a pig's ear of it.

Well, it took some very harsh words from a couple I met during my first few months in Norfolk to send me on a new trajectory. The couple, who were in their late fifties and had taken me under their wing, sent me an email saying "You really should stop being a victim… get out of your own pity party." There it was, in black and white, written by the dominating male chauvinist husband who obviously believed it was his *God-given* right to lecture me, seeing as he was a life coach. How dare he! Yes, I had cancelled lunch with them after yet another disastrous online date the night before, but I was horrified at his blunt words and sent an email straight back, telling him and his wife what a judgemental, freaky, bible-bashing pair of know-it-alls they were and how they had no right to be so judgemental of me, especially not having known me for long. I drowned my sorrows in another bottle of wine and indulged in my "pity party".

They may have been outspoken, and the words may have been a little harsh, but it turned out they were right. I grew to thank that couple despite never seeing them again because it was the catalyst to start my journey of making *change* happen. I was going to turn my life around and become a far better version of myself by learning how to modify my behaviours and reactions one step at a time. My father had always told me "a leopard doesn't change its spots"; that we can't change our behaviour or who we are. But I know this to be untrue. Change is by no means easy but with my new awareness of the need to do so, it was the best place to start.

I had moved away from Surrey to leave behind the heartache and dramas of my previous life, and yet here I was creating more of the same. I had thought I could run away from it all and just expect life to change, but I now realised that it was *me* who had to change first. It was time to put down my heavy rucksack that was carrying all the pain of my previous life, and become the *type* of person that attracted the calm and peaceful life that I so craved. I decided to flick up my rear-view mirror and start to focus on the road ahead of me now, with its new landscape of unending possibilities and a brighter future.

I also needed to come to terms with being single and shrug off the shackles of relationship dependency, something inherent in my family. Sadly, I had never got to grips with being on my own, believing happiness was only achievable by being with a partner to hold me up. That was why I had made poor choices with my previous two husbands, desperate to be with someone and fill the void of loneliness, a sure sign of lack of self-worth. Yes, if I wanted a peaceful life with no more dramas, if I wanted calm in my life, then *I* needed to change. This was the only sure way to find happiness and peace. It was one of life's toughest lessons for me.

So, with a new shelf of self-development books and drinking habits nipped in the bud, I finally opened a new chapter. I let go of the voice which said I wasn't good enough, and tuned in to a different frequency where I began to venture further and further out of my comfort zone.

It was on this new journey of self-discovery that I happened across my Mr Right. Alright, so my journey of complete independence was fairly short-lived, probably no more than a year, but Martin truly enhanced my journey and helped speed up the course that I was now on. He gave me the safety in which to emerge from my chrysalis a new, better version of me, without the fear of being judged or criticised by others, just praised and encouraged to blossom. It was a case of the "right man at the right time".

When you truly change, there are subtle nuances that emerge. I found laughter in my life for the first time. I believe you have to be truly free to laugh and yes, it really is so good for the soul. Martin and I laugh, and I mean really laugh. I hadn't even realised that it had been missing in my life until we met! Thirteen years later he can still make me dissolve into a hysterical fit of giggles at the smallest of things that other people just can't relate to, and I don't mean just a snigger or the obligatory chuckle at a friend's joke. Oh no, I mean belly-breaking, knicker-wetting, uncontrollable laughing until tears are streaming down my face and I'm begging him to stop. We are intrinsically connected in our child-like way of thinking, best shown in the fun we have putting on silly voices, commentating on Mabel and Chester's thoughts or perhaps a couple of random pigeons sitting on a telegraph pole, all in true Johnny Morris style. (Anyone remember Animal Magic or am I showing my age here?)

The new confident me started to try new things I had never done before and learnt to embrace life in exciting new ways. I began my own business with a brand called Tropic Skincare, a direct sales business which turned out to be one of the best decisions of my life (aside from changing my mind and agreeing to get married again). It allowed me to escape from a secretarial job that was unfulfilling, as well as my horrible bully of a boss who made my life a misery. It was perfect timing. I became my own boss for the first time in my life.

I had to pinch myself sometimes, as this once under-confident, socially phobic, middle-aged woman was suddenly in strange women's houses giving presentations and holding court for entire evenings whilst selling beauty products. I didn't have to fake my confidence either, I genuinely started to enjoy what I was doing and loved meeting new people. There was no longer the inhibited awkwardness of feeling that people could see through me, or the need to fill every gap in a conversation with fumbling small talk. There was no fear of worrying what others thought of me; I was free to just be me.

It wasn't long before I started to make new friends with customers, hosts of parties and then ladies who decided to come and join my team. We soon became a Tropic family, and I discovered a new passion in life, motivating and supporting others! It turned out I had quite a flair for it too, winning trips to exotic locations; Lapland, Mauritius, a safari in South Africa. I was having the time of my life.

I had always felt myself to be a bit of a loner in life (well you *do* when you have social phobia), preferring to keep myself to myself and not really making the effort to make new friends. So this new lifestyle was incredibly empowering for me. I had never realised the importance of people in bringing colour, shape, and flavour to life! It was as if the HD button was turned on, making the world a much brighter place.

'You're going on holiday on your own?' I remember my mum saying to me when I won the first trip to Lapland.

'No, Mum, with about two hundred other Tropic women.'

'But Martin isn't going with you?'

'No, Mum, we can't take our partners.'

'You're going on your own then.'

'No, Mum, I'm going with Tropic.'

'You're going on your own then; well, I must say I think you're very brave.'

She was right, this *was* brave for me. I'd never ventured abroad on a trip like this before, but it was to be the first of many, and I certainly wasn't alone.

'You go into complete strangers' houses and run parties?'

'Yes, Mum, I give demonstrations in people's houses; women I've met at other pampers.'

There was a stunned silence.

'I wonder if you're actually my daughter these days!'

Chapter4

Dilemma

Martin sat outside the operating theatre keeping vigil for the entire seven-hour operation, terrified that he might lose me. When the surgeons finally came out of theatre, they were surprised to find him still sitting in the same spot where they'd left him. They gave him a reassuring pat on the shoulder as they passed him, telling him that all had gone well.

As I slowly came round from the anaesthetic, it was like waking up from the deepest of sleeps, a peaceful sleep which I hadn't had in what seemed like a lifetime. I felt instant relief when I realised where I was; I had survived, I was still here. The first face I saw was Martin's; it showed such relief, and his loving smile told me I was safe. I was meant to be here, it had all been lies. The world wasn't going to end.

Apparently, there were some immediate signs of the psychosis lifting when I came out of the anaesthetic. I seemed kinder, less scared, with a little more awareness of the real world. Perhaps the anaesthetic pressed some sort of reset button in my brain, starting the process of coming back to the world of the living, back to sanity.

I was taken to a small room shared by three other patients on Gately Ward, an orthopaedic ward on the top floor of the hospital. Other than some awareness of the window with the occasional bit of blue sky, all that I could see was the white panelled ceiling and faces when they peered over me.

My world became a blur of drugs, pain management and sleep: observations were done every two hours, checking my blood pressure and temperature, blood tests were continuously taken, cannulas were changed, compression socks put on. There were endless tests of one sort or another and I felt pulled from pillar to post, my arm black and blue from all the needle punctures.

Every three hours I was to have something called a "log roll" which involved four nurses strategically positioned to gently roll me on one side with minimal impact on my spine. The purpose of this was to check for any marks that could be a sign of bedsores, which were now a risk as I couldn't move. The entire Gately Ward must have heard the first one: as the nurses rolled my body towards them, it caused a horrific sensation of my back being left behind on the bed, making me yell obscenities and wail like an injured animal. Once my back was checked for sores I was then rolled back again, which was equally as painful. Now either I got used to this, or the pain got easier because my groans soon decreased, and these rolls became the new norm during my hospital stay.

The call button was tucked into my pillow so that I could reach it if I needed a nurse. The response when I pressed it was far from instant. It would trigger a red light to flash above the entrance to the room and you could hear the repetitive buzzing noise out in the nurses' station. It could take up to half an hour for someone to respond, even longer at night, which made me feel like I was being ignored, although it was more likely due to a lack of staff. The buzzing sound would irritate me and, what with the continuous wail of sirens as the next ambulance left the hospital, I'm surprised that I managed to drift in and out of sleep.

Whilst it was a relief that the horrific nightmares didn't continue in my head at the same intensity as before, there was a period of being caught between two worlds, a bit like the hypnopompic stage of sleep when your consciousness is "coming to"— ironically, the stage that is vulnerable to sleep paralysis although my body was already partly paralysed. As I was stirring back to full sanity, part of me didn't want to wake up and face what had happened.

My only real memory of severe pain was on the second night after my operation. I could feel waves of deep pain in my lower back which reminded me of labour contractions. I think I have a fairly low pain threshold, and I confess to being quite a wimp, even though I did survive childbirth three times, once without an epidural too. There was no luxury of an epidural here though... I repeatedly pressed the button to call for help and with no nurses coming to my rescue, I began to whimper.

A lovely lady in the bed opposite me was like my guardian angel watching over me that night. She was extremely reassuring as she comforted me with her kind words each time I moaned. I couldn't see her, since lying completely horizontal and unable to move, if I tried to look down, all I could see was my size 34Gs! But she spoke to me as if I was a dear friend of hers and told me to "hang on in there". She pressed her buzzer in an attempt to escalate the urgency, but still no nurse arrived. I felt panicked by the increasing waves of unbearable pain and started to cry out for help as she continued to try to soothe me.

By the time nurses finally came I was blubbing my eyes out and crying like a small child, begging for more pain relief, but they couldn't give me any since I was already on the highest dose. I remember getting so distressed by this that I begged to speak to Martin. I was advised not to call as it was nearly midnight, but I wouldn't take no for an answer, and after waking him up in a daze I hollered down the phone how I needed him here with me *now*, that it was worse than having a baby and the pain was like nothing I had ever experienced in my entire life. He must have felt so helpless since he couldn't come and visit during the night, plus he was trying to manage our café by day, poor chap! He was doing everything he could, but fixing my pain was outside of his power.

I somehow got through those bleak early days on Gately Ward, with the physical pain seeming to compete with the mental. The anti-psychotic meds were already starting to kick in but I wasn't out of the woods quite yet. I glared at nurses silently, still suspicious of what was happening, unable to communicate like the old me, whilst trying to take in my current dilemma. It was a huge shock being thrown into this new world of pain, trying to absorb the fact that I had broken my back and, worse still, that I had had another shameful episode of psychosis.

Now, something I have always found incredibly hard to disclose is the fact that I have suffered episodes of psychosis in my life prior to this traumatic incident; four to be precise. Only my husband and very close family know this about me. It has always been a brief episode (thank God) and not related to any other condition such as schizophrenia or bipolar disorder, which I'm not sure makes it any easier to accept. It's almost more shocking perhaps, that a mentally "well" person can go so horribly wrong; to go from sanity to insanity in the blink of an eye. It has certainly made it harder to know when it's coming, that's for sure.

The last incident had been in January 2017 – prior to that, there hadn't been an incident for nine years, a long enough gap for me to believe it wasn't going to happen again. But then the shock of finding out that Martin had been financially unfaithful to me had been a trigger.

Honesty is a big thing with me. Maybe it stems from being told as a child that the little white dots on your fingernails show how many lies you've told. Each time you tell a lie to someone you get a white dot for the whole world to see. Well, I now know it's probably a sign of calcium deficiency, but I still can't lie even to this day. Some people seem to do it so easily though. I brought some trust baggage from my pre-Norfolk years after ending a relationship that obliterated my trust (ironically) due to financial indiscretion on a very large scale. Perhaps this exacerbated my need for mutual honesty, but Martin knows how trust is a core value for me and he knew his misdemeanour would cause an immeasurable amount of stress.

Martin had been hiding his problems with money for some time, building up a stack of debts and borrowing from his mum. As his debt built, the more he lied to me. It was mainly a case of living beyond his means; there was no gambling or other addiction, but more a case of money "burning a hole in his pocket".

Things started to unravel when I found a receipt in the bottom of a drawer for some work that had been carried out on my car nearly eighteen months earlier, with a threatening letter demanding that it be paid for. This was followed by discovering an unpaid tax bill for his decorating business which I was assured had now been dealt with. I chose to believe him when he promised me that there was nothing else. So, maybe I'm a bit naïve, but I was utterly shocked to come home a week later to find him sitting on the sofa ready to disclose the full extent of his misdemeanour. The amount was almost irrelevant. I would have been able to handle the debt, it was a problem we could have faced together; but to know he had been rushing to the post before me in order to hide his credit card statements and other demands? That he was deliberately "hiding" how much he had been spending and borrowing from his mother whilst continuing with life as if nothing was wrong? That was too much to bear. Obviously, he knew this, and had packed up his things prior to his big disclosure and then walked out on me, taking our dog Chester and leaving me in complete shock. He took matters into his own hands, believing that I would throw him out anyway.

Two weeks later I suffered a psychosis which lasted about three weeks, most of which was spent in a psychiatric unit, an experience that took me to hell and back. I was diagnosed with a stress-induced psychotic episode, the same as the previous times it had happened. However, in my endeavours to keep this hidden, people were told that I had had a "nervous breakdown". Nobody need know I had been in "that" hospital.

Once I was put on the correct meds which gradually pulled me out of the psychosis, I was allowed home, where, with utter determination and driven by fear of being uncovered, I pushed myself back to "normal" life, leaving the edges of the horrific nightmare to recede into the depths of my mind. It is almost the embarrassment of the episode and the feeling I've done something wrong which pushes me to recover so quickly.

Martin had moved back in to our home whilst I had been in the hospital; partly to be there for my daughter Chloe but also because he was sofa hopping in friends' houses. I wasn't in a fit state of mind to complain and appreciated having his support when I got home. He had also visited me whilst I had been in hospital, guilt-ridden that he had caused me to be there.

I was back working within a few weeks, albeit feeling a little shaken and certainly not having given myself time to fully recuperate. I don't think it helps that I come from a family who brush things under the carpet and shuffle awkwardly in their chair if you mention the words "mental health". This, and other stigma linked to psychosis, forced me to keep it as my own grubby little secret. I think I actually convinced myself that if I could forget it had happened, then it was as if it never had, and Martin and my family had never been witness to it either.

Having a psychotic experience is, without doubt, the worst thing that has ever happened to me. I don't know if it's the same for other sufferers, but initially, it starts as an enlightening revelation, where I'm shown the secret to life, an epiphany which my brain soon turns into panic and fear since it is like an overload of information that is too great to handle. This is followed by what can only be described as all my worst nightmares coming alive one by one in my head. Every thought, dream, and nightmare since childhood springs into action and becomes my new reality, leaving me in a catatonic, confused state. It is truly awful, not just for me, but for those closest to me.

So, with Martin and I back together, and working hard at the trust issues in our marriage, the last traumatic episode was kept firmly under wraps just like the previous times. There are no tell-tale signs after an episode; no nervous twitches, give-away white dots or branding across my forehead, so thankfully my mental health secret has always been easy to keep hidden and my perfectly sane persona kept safely intact.

I am so grateful that my psychosis is not a chronic condition. Whilst I say I am "mentally well", that I don't suffer with any other chronic mental health issues, it hasn't always been that way. I have suffered depression in my past (in my pre-Norfolk years) but have discovered a way to keep it at bay, largely credited to the amount of self-development I have undertaken (not to imply that depression can always be resolved in this way, of course). Through my journey of change, I have developed skills to stop myself sliding down the slippery slope into darkness, halting the depression monster before it gets its claws in and tries to drag me down into its pain and lies. Even when I have difficulties with my daughters, which could so easily be something to lure me back into its clutches, I find myself resilient these days. I still have ups and downs, like we all do… but if I feel low for any reason, I usually bounce back within a day or two. Yes, I have become quite the expert at putting things in a box if I can't resolve or fix them and firmly shutting the lid. Psychosis, however, seems to be like a jack in the box, slowly wound up and bursting out unpredictably to scare me from time to time.

I work in a female-dominated business where I support many women who struggle with confidence issues as well as mental health issues, in particular, anxiety. It is an awful condition and one I don't feel I could cope with based on my experience of it… which is a brief but intense meeting as a precursor before my episodes of psychosis, and that is enough! I can see how debilitating it is, as are other conditions that affect our mental wellbeing. I love to help build the confidence and self-belief of these women in my team and often listen to their issues and difficulties whilst helping them step out of their comfort zone to grow their business and achieve success, which has been so rewarding, and hopefully empowering for them.

So, to those in the outside world who know nothing of my brief psychotic episodes, I'm the kind of person who seems like they really have their shit together in life. Not someone who in true all or nothing style, literally goes "bang" inside their head, which makes them so crazy they end up in a psychiatric hospital. But what was I to do now? Not only did I have to contend with the realisation that I had suffered another episode of psychosis, but also the fact that it had left a cataclysmic amount of damage in its wake.

Something told me that I wouldn't be rushing back to work this time. A broken back was a clear tell-tale sign that I would never be able to hide. Can you see the dilemma I was faced with? I didn't know when or how, but I knew that this shameful episode could not be brushed under the carpet. People would ask, 'What on earth happened?'

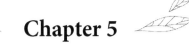

Chapter 5

The Trigger

It was in June 2019, just one month before the accident, when I finally decided I had to face up to the one vice I had in life, Nicorette Gum! I was riding high on recent success with my business and other thinigs, so felt it was the right time to address the one weakness that I had clearly been ignoring. It was a habit so ingrained over the years that I was mostly unaware I was even chewing it. The first thing I would do on waking in the morning would be to put one of the sugar-coated little white squares of nicotine into my mouth before even getting out of bed. Sad to say there was a piece in my mouth nearly twenty-four hours a day (although I did remove it when I went to sleep). A business colleague who was also a therapist had once said to me that there must be some insecurity or a past issue that kept me hooked on it. Perhaps she was right, but I had chosen to ignore the comment, to give it no further thought and keep my nicotine habit safely buried under the carpet. After all, I didn't drink or have any other real vices.

But then months slipped into years and, in fact, for about eight years since giving up cigarettes, I had been chewing around ten to fifteen pieces of 2 mg gum a day, the lowest strength available, which also served to convince me it wasn't a habit that needed addressing. But deep down I knew I was becoming a slave to it. My dependency meant I would feel a sense of panic if I ran out and didn't have any in the house, just like cigarettes did in the past. It started to play on my mind that I might go into old age still chewing and addicted to the damn stuff, so, as I was striving to become the best version of myself with the help of my latest books on personal growth, I decided to find a therapist to help with this as I felt I couldn't do it alone. A bit of added support would only increase my chances of success with this surreptitious addiction.

After much research, I found a local lady that helped with a whole host of things like depression, anxiety, and addictions. She seemed to have an adequate list of qualifications and many years' experience, so I decided to go with her.

Janet was a middle-aged lady who came across friendly enough in our first Zoom call; I found her easy to talk to despite being separated by technology. I guessed she was a bit older than me, maybe even in her sixties. She had allowed her short hair to turn naturally grey and I imagined her to be a very organised and self-disciplined individual, perhaps a little square. But this straight-laced character seemed the perfect choice to give me the guidance and help I was seeking.

The purpose of my first appointment with Janet was for her to learn what I needed help with, and for us to get to know each other, to make me feel comfortable with the whole process. She listened to my chewing gum dilemma and was unsure, like me, whether it was a chewing or nicotine addiction, but either way it needed to be resolved. Freud would have had a field day analysing my oral fixation, seemingly always having something in my mouth, be it gum or food!

Janet explained that we would use a new kind of treatment called BWRT or Brain Wiring Recursive Therapy, which was a relatively new treatment, only discovered in the last couple of years, but very successful. Known for being the Google queen in our home, I was straight on the internet after our appointment!

It uses natural psychological processes to recondition neural pathways in the brain that lead to unwanted behaviour by stopping and rerouting the brain's natural response to anything traumatic or not understood in its tracks.

I remember Janet using the analogy that the door in my mind which usually led me to reach for the gum would be gone, plastered over, that there would be a new door further along the wall for my thought processes to enter without the impulse to reach for the gum anymore. Wow! It sounded like a magic solution. I asked if I would be hypnotized, intrigued and slightly excited by all this. She said categorically that it wasn't the same as hypnosis, which I thought strange since it certainly sounded like it to me.

She proceeded to ask me lots of questions, wanting to know all the reasons why I wanted to give up, asking me to visualise myself in the future once free of gum. I could clearly see the new me free from the gum, smiling and laughing whilst talking to Martin with a gin and tonic in hand on a summer's evening sitting on our wicker chairs in the garden, with no mouth chomping at the bit! She told me to focus on my taste here, and I immediately imagined how refreshing the gin and tonic tasted; perhaps my taste buds would improve? I truly imagined myself being free from it, whilst Janet was busy making notes since she would be using all my answers to recite back to me during the BWRT treatment in a kind of repetitive loop later on. This would be in our next appointment the following week, which I felt strangely impatient for now.

Janet then asked me to describe and visualise my fears, one of which was growing old, so I pictured myself still chewing the gum with my false teeth in some old people's home. Then after thinking about the prospect of my teeth collapsing with the constant pressure, Janet asked if there were any other fears. I scratched around in my head, thinking.

'Falling apart,' I said. At that moment I had a very brief but sharp flashback that took me by complete surprise, to the episode of psychosis that I had buried at the back of my mind; to the time when I was in the psychiatric unit just a few years before and a dark nightmare of being chased by evil. What relevance did that have to this though? None! Bizarre…

'What do you mean by falling apart?' she asked. It was too difficult to explain, something I would *never* want to discuss.

'Kind of unravelling,' I added, a bit confused. Well, psychosis is exactly like that. It feels as though somebody, or something, unravels your brain like a large piece of knitting being pulled apart. 'Not being able to cope without it?' I quickly added as I pushed the thought away and brought my focus back to the present. Janet assured me that the

BWRT would be far easier than perhaps I was imagining and to try not to worry.

The meeting came to a close. This had all been the setup for our next appointment, the one where Janet would work her magic on me, and I would finally be free of gum. We booked the zoom call for a few days after my birthday on the 2 July and I felt slightly disappointed that I wouldn't get to meet her in person, since I quite enjoyed nattering away, telling her about my recent success with my Tropic business and the tribulations of Mabel's naughty escapades, information I'm sure she didn't actually need, but it's good to talk!

I had learnt to manage stress and I had such a peaceful life nowadays, so why that dark nightmare had flashed into my head whilst talking to Janet, I do not know. I didn't give it another thought and looked forward to my next appointment with her, although I had my dreaded 52nd birthday to get through first.

I'm not too keen on birthdays these days. I haven't fully settled into my fifties, and don't think I will anytime soon. Just like my father, I now felt the time had come in life where birthdays work better in reverse, getting one year younger each year and heading back towards the allure of youth.

My other feeling of gloom surrounding my birthday was the unwelcoming thought of not receiving a card from my daughter, Steph. Stupid really, since I should be used to it by now; but there's nothing that can cut to the core of a mother's insecurity and guilt quite like a child not acknowledging your birthday. I have three daughters; the complexities of which can be like a Molotov cocktail at times. Martin and I joke that if ever all three were to announce they were coming home for Christmas (highly unlikely as there's always one daughter who has either fallen out with another— or with me), we would leave a turkey ready prepped in the oven for them and jump on the next plane out of the country. But jesting aside, the pain I feel as a mother with the complexities of my relationships with my girls can be very harrowing at times, often making me feel disempowered and impotent.

Sadly, on the Saturday of my birthday it turned out to be a double whammy. It wasn't just one daughter who failed to send me a card, but two! This added fuel to my despondency, compounding my negative feelings. It was like a piercing knife through the heart, stirring up that familiar grief inside.

Now my youngest daughter, Chloe, was at home after finishing her first year at uni. She gave me a sheepish look as she walked into the lounge and checked all the cards on the mantelpiece.

'What... no card from Amy either?' she asked, as she gave me her card and present. She knew I was upset, and I felt she was trying to compensate with her abundance of hugs and kisses. I owed it to her to get my head out of my pain, stop wallowing in my self-pity, and focus on the positive. I tried to pretend I wasn't overly bothered and focused on the gorgeous rose gold water bottle she gave me and the beautiful card with its words of appreciation. We were going to Rocky Bottom, a fish restaurant, with Martin and his mother that night. There was a lot to be thankful for.

It can be so annoying that Martin knows me better than I know myself sometimes and he instantly recognized the pain in my eyes when he got home from work. He tried to reassure me that there would be a logical reason for "cardgate".

'I'm sure they just forgot and will text or call you later. Perhaps their cards will come in the post on Monday? Now focus on the daughter you have right here, focus on the now.' I knew he was right and tried to put it out of my mind and stop torturing myself.

By the following Tuesday, it was painfully obvious that no cards were coming, and it was preying on my mind again. I sat at my desk in my office, staring out of the window, unable to focus. If I confronted the situation, it might make more sense, or possibly highlight to them how unkind they had been not sending a card. It shouldn't go unquestioned, surely? That just made me a victim, didn't it? On the other hand, what if they had genuinely forgotten; they deserved the opportunity to apologise, didn't they?

As I sat staring at the little box labelled "cards for compassion" sitting on my desk, cards with daily kindness quotes on that had been a gift from Amy, I plucked up the courage to send them both a message. I was cut to the core with Amy's curt reply which indicated she felt I deserved no less, that I had always been a let-down as a mother and that she would be a far better mother to her children one day. Steph, however, responded with an apology saying that she had been busy and had just forgotten. There is always one daughter with whom I'm out of favour, possibly even two on occasion. I dread the day I should ever reach the hat trick!

I re-read Amy's message, stupidly allowing myself to be drawn in. I can look back on it now and see it for what it was, but at the time I allowed it to stab me in the heart and took what she said as a personal attack on my very being. Thankfully Chloe wasn't around to see me blubbing and dissolving into a teary mess, as she had gone down to Surrey to visit family. My number one daughter, my baby bear, genuinely loathed me so much that she couldn't acknowledge my birthday and I, just like always, didn't understand why.

It was poor Martin, who was up to his ears in egg and bacon orders in our café, who got the full extent of my blubbering down the phone. The one thing left in my life that could bring back insecurities and make me dissolve like this was my girls.

In true Sir Galahad style, Martin suddenly appeared at our front door, having left someone in charge of cooking to get home to me. He sat in the lounge whilst I hysterically poured out how much it hurt. I read Amy's text to him and explained how I didn't understand how my own flesh and blood could be so unkind to me, how he had been completely wrong with his optimism and that there was no way to justify the lack of kindness or respect in not sending me a card.

Martin hates seeing in me in pain and yet handles it so well. Having listened and gently coaxed my feelings out of me, mimicking the best of counsellors, an hour later he gave me an action plan for the rest of the day and made me promise to not message or text anymore. He truly helped me to let it go, briefly reminding me that it wasn't good for me to get stressed. I knew he was right, as always, but each time I have had to distance myself from my daughters, unable to say or do anything to resolve things, it is incredibly painful for me and eats away a little piece of my heart.

Now as I have said before, wallowing in self-pity is not my thing. It serves no purpose. Guilt also serves no purpose. Wasted emotions, wasted energy. I needed to get my mind back in gear. I could handle this. First though, as I was so shattered, drained by my emotions, I went to have a sleep and recharge my batteries. I then forced myself to grow up and get on with it, making something for Martin's dinner and walking the dogs to force any lingering thoughts away from my mind to do with both daughters. I found my calm again and another scar started to form over the wound as I firmly shut the lid on the box.

Two days later I had my much-anticipated appointment with Janet. Despite never wanting to give up the gum before, I was quite excited by this new challenge and intrigued as to how this BWRT thing worked. I was back to my usual bouncy self, laughing and joking as we greeted each other. I briefly mentioned how it had been a bit of a "stressy" week, and Janet politely asked if I wanted to rearrange. I refused and said I was fine, that I was well accustomed to having problems with my daughters. I took a deep breath. The week had shaken me emotionally, but I was alright now. I had to do this for me.

Janet asked me to tell her my worst fears again. I repeated what I had said before, about my teeth falling out and growing old, but also added this time that I feared mouth cancer or possibly even tongue cancer too.

'Any other fears?' she asked. I thought about it.

'Falling apart...' And then it happened again, a brief flash of that horrific dark nightmare. For God's sake, it was like when you're told not to think of pink elephants; part of me didn't want to *ever* remember what had happened, but the thought of psychosis snuck back in there. I think it was the word *fear* perhaps, that triggered this unwelcome memory to briefly flash through my mind. I flinched before coming back to the moment and giving Janet the other examples of fear whilst she made finishing touches to her notes.

What followed was really very bizarre!

First, I was told to put my gum in the bin (yes, I was actually chewing a piece at that moment) and then Janet asked me to close my eyes. She proceeded to recite sentences in a repetitive, rhythmical manner with all my answers jumbled up. It was almost like a chant, which got faster and faster, interspersing descriptions of the past me, the current me and the future me. I was only catching snippets of what she was saying but it included all the fears I had mentioned to her and the visualisations I had described to her. As she sped up, repeating the words more urgently, I could feel my eyeballs start to flicker uncontrollably and wondered if she could see this through my closed lids from across the screen. In hindsight, she was probably looking down reading her notes and not even looking at me. My eyes began watering and the light through my office window seemed particularly bright, making me tighten my lids further. I found myself wanting to ask if this was normal but was worried that if I interrupted her, perhaps the treatment wouldn't work. I was quite overwhelmed at how weird this was, and my heartbeat reflected this, its beat almost rising into my throat. This intensity carried on for roughly two to three minutes and then it was over... Janet stopped.

It was strangely quiet. Janet asked me to take a deep breath and open my eyes. I felt immense relief. But then, as I opened my eyelids, it felt like my eyeballs were still shaking, only they weren't, it was inside my head, a sensation like something had shaken my brain, leaving it scrambled and very wobbly, punch drunk perhaps. I felt slightly alarmed, but not wanting to appear weird or complaining in any way, I squinted at Janet and just smiled. I couldn't easily describe how I felt and merely told her that my eyes had started shaking during the treatment. She was non-reactive, saying everyone responded differently and it was nothing to be worried about. She warned that I may be tired, and to take it easy for the remainder of the day and that was it. We said goodbye, and her job was done.

But why hadn't she pre-warned me that this could happen? Why hadn't she even noticed the jerking of my eyes? I had a slightly uneasy feeling stirring in my stomach and knew that something just wasn't quite right.

The switch had been flicked.

Chapter 6

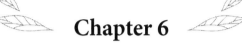

Slipping

I awoke the following morning after my appointment with a huge knot in my stomach. The anxiety was still there and was reminiscent of the feeling I used to get as a child when I was homesick and felt panicky at being away from the safety of my parents. I used to cry to go home when staying overnight with friends or even grandparents, but I couldn't do that now, I *was* home! For goodness sake, why was my brain overthinking it? I had merely had a therapy treatment and given up nicotine gum. End of. But would this anxiety pass in a day or two? I couldn't cope if not. It was like an intruder had entered my very being, giving me this unsettling feeling. Unfortunately, I had forgotten that I had felt something like this in the past, as a precursor; I failed to see the warning signs. But then, why would I? I hadn't received any earth-shattering news; I hadn't experienced anything that had been clearly stress-related, had I?

I checked my emails to see if Janet had replied to my late-night message.

Hi Janet, I have had a cracking headache since our session this afternoon, which I'm aware may just be from the tension

I've had this week. However, I've been strangely obsessing about trying to work out what's happening in my head rather than going with the flow. No massive withdrawal or falling apart at the seams but I seem to be constantly thinking about keeping my thoughts in check. I kind of think of "it" (the gum) as "he who cannot be named". I couldn't even describe it to my husband or say phrases like "giving up gum" when describing our appointment to him… it makes no sense because I can't use the word "gum"— it's as if it's a taboo word now. Does this make any sense to you? The moment where I think there could possibly be a craving trying to get through, I get a scrambled feeling in my head, like a power surge, so I take a deep breath and then it's gone. Is this normal? I hope my brain will be okay when I wake up tomorrow but something's not right. Many thanks for your support in this life-changing event. Nikki xx

Wow. There's quite a lot of confusion in this email, and "*he who cannot be named*"? That feels rather sinister and gives me goosebumps when I read it back now.

I found myself trying to overcompensate so as not to reveal my new anxiety to Martin and Chloe. I didn't want them to think anything was wrong, to worry about me. I felt torn inside; on the one hand wanting to cry out and say I didn't feel right, but then on the other, I felt I had perhaps done something irresponsible by having the BWRT, seeing as it was a new treatment, or by having the appointment with someone I hadn't even met. I felt that maybe I was a failure by responding to it like this. No, I needed to sort myself out, pull up my big girl pants and rise above this. I wanted to show them and, in fact, *everyone,* my success at giving up the gum.

The brain fog increased as the day went on. I couldn't focus properly and was starting to feel a little detached from myself, as though I was looking in from the outside. Janet briefly called me in response to my messages and when I explained that I had some anxiety she said to see how I fared over the weekend, and if I felt I needed a further BWRT to help with the anxiety, to contact her the following week and we could hook up for another appointment. But why would I do that? Apart from the cost, why would I do something *again* that had given me this headache in the first place?

I had a pamper experience to do that evening for a dear friend of mine who knows me well. I struggled to put on my usual display of confidence and professionalism with her guests. My opening spiel, which I have been rattling off for many years and know like the back of my hand, seemed to evade me. I stammered my way through my speech, becoming increasingly aware that I wasn't flowing like usual. It was a bit like a bad dream; the kind where you wake up on stage in the middle of a play where you haven't learnt your lines and you don't know how you got there!

I couldn't relax the whole evening and felt paranoid that people could see through my pretence; I was treading water. But thankfully most of the guests had not met me before and I hoped wouldn't meet me again. My friend didn't ask me if anything was wrong when I said goodbye to her, so I presumed I had got away with it. Nobody had seen the internal struggle as I tried to hang on to the fading threads of my remaining self. I was exhausted. When I got home it was around ten o'clock, so I went straight to bed, avoiding any interaction with Martin, praying that this head fog would be gone when I woke up in the morning. It had felt like one of the longest days of my life.

The next day was the same, followed by the next. But I was functioning on a level where I was able to excuse my slightly altered behaviour by just being tired, a bit under par, or not feeling quite right. Martin was so preoccupied with the café that we had recently acquired that my behaviour seemed to be going unnoticed.

I somehow managed to do a *live* on Facebook a couple of days later. I was quite adept at pressing the little red record button which instantly allowed everyone online to see me. I had prepped well and written everything down that I wanted to talk about, practising a few times before I started. I wanted to tell everyone about the BWRT and how I was conquering my addiction, which hopefully would increase my algorithm on Facebook. I laughed and joked as I chatted about the strange experience, telling everyone how it had made my head feel like scrambled eggs! I can't believe how I went into great detail, sharing the whole experience with no idea of what was coming.

My confidence was rapidly decreasing, to the extent that I felt I had to cancel the upcoming training for my team. There was no way I could train them when my thoughts were becoming even more disorganised. I couldn't focus and knew I wouldn't present with confidence. They couldn't see their motivational leader like this! I would postpone until the following week when I would hopefully be feeling better.

I decided to tell Martin that I was struggling with anxiety and he confirmed what I was thinking; that it was probably just nicotine withdrawal, and I should contact Janet again in the morning if I still didn't feel right.

The following day my anxiety was still increasing, now with waves of what felt like impending panic attacks. My appetite was dissipating plus my sleep was becoming disturbed; I could only sleep for a short period of time before waking with panic and then I was too scared to go back to sleep. I emailed Janet. It had been nearly a week since our appointment; I heard nothing back.

For the life of me, I have no idea how, but I managed to drag myself to a Tropic Leaders Event for the next two days. I continued putting on my act and breathing through the internal panic, but my feet were paddling like crazy underwater. It was exhausting trying to stay afloat.

I'm pretty sure the two teamies that I went with must have found me weird and distant, unlike my usual self. The sensation reminded me of the experience I had in my teens of smoking weed, which I hated... a bit spaced out, a feeling of not being myself and generally not fully "with it".

My personality reverted to the old pre-Norfolk me when I struggled with social phobia. Thankfully I was rescued from too much social interaction by the amazing Susie Ma and her crew, who drew the focus with an amazing presentation. It was only in the lunch break that I had to socialise for a short while. I awkwardly tried to make conversation but couldn't absorb a single word that people were saying to me. I take my hat off to people that struggle with anxiety in their daily lives. I can fully understand why they would avoid going out or doing things; it was such a struggle just trying to appear normal and hold a conversation.

In one awkward moment, where I was aware of the pressure to speak, I relayed the experience of the BWRT treatment, almost as if to excuse my "weirdness". I explained that it had done something "funny" to my head and scrambled my brain a bit but thank God I wasn't chewing the Nicorette Gum anymore, eh? I described the strange process in detail, saying that Janet had "been speaking in tongues". My friend, who happened to be a pastor's wife, looked a bit taken aback.

'Nikki, you should be very careful, I don't like the sound of this,' she said, like a warning that I may have got involved with some kind of cult or dark force. I tried to ignore her reaction; after all, what was done was done, but I think it may have amplified that foreboding feeling in my stomach. Oh God, what if I'd done something stupid and Janet had placed a spell on me or conjured up some evil spirit!

Later that night at the Gala party, I acted completely out of character and got absolutely legless. In truth, I'd had a few drinks in my room for Dutch courage whilst getting ready but it only served to make me feel even more spaced out, as though I was on the outside of the playground looking in on everyone else partying and having a good time. The more I drank the worse I felt. Suddenly I was a stranger in this world. I didn't belong and I just wanted to go home.

As everyone started to get more drunk and enjoy themselves, I felt myself becoming increasingly upset, unable to cope, and worse still, unable to hide it. I didn't want to be here, I wanted to go home. The next best thing was to go back to my hotel room where I was staying on my own, so I left.

The conference centre was within a huge complex, with cinemas, shops or restaurants on every level. It was like a giant maze and I was hopelessly lost. I kept hitting a dead end as I went up and down the escalators, baffled by how an entire hotel had just "disappeared" into thin air. I must have been a sight for sore eyes as I staggered around, a drunken mess, mascara streaming down my face, bleary-eyed with a sheer look of panic on my face. I could feel the alcohol swirling in my stomach and the ground seemed to be swaying with my double vision. I hadn't got myself wrecked like this for at least a decade.

I felt an increasing sense of fear, building like a wave, and then it happened. The wave came crashing down in the form of a full-on panic attack. The hustle and bustle of people moving around me in different directions up and down escalators, the brightness of the lights, the cacophony of amplified sounds and me feeling hopelessly lost in a maze with no way out. I phoned Martin with my heart pounding so hard I could feel it pulsating in my ears. I sobbed down the phone, barely able to breathe, telling him that I didn't know what was wrong with me.

At this point, two lovely Tropic ladies recognised me from the party and asked if I was alright. They had spotted me trying to put my hotel room key into the car parking machine! I dissolved into tears on the spot and cried like a lost child. Thankfully they were staying in the same hotel as me and, after saying goodbye to a now very concerned Martin, kindly took an arm each, guiding me back to the safety of my hotel room. I am eternally grateful to those two ladies. I will never forget their kindness and how they stayed with me back in my room until I seemed settled.

It didn't quite end there though. Once they left, I couldn't comprehend sleep. I lay there crying and panicking with circular thoughts getting stuck in my head about how my daughters hated me. I sent a message in our team WhatsApp group to the other leaders.

"Can someone please come and help me as I'm having a panic attack."

I was drawing attention to myself now, but I was feeling traumatised by the panic attack and scared about being alone in my room, feeling like I had when I was little, being left in a hotel room alone with my older brother whilst my parents were out dining with their friends.

When help arrived, I just dissolved into a weepy mess, indulging in all the heartbreak of how my daughters ignored my birthday and how they hated me so much but there was nothing I could do to fix it. I seemed to be pinning all the blame for being in this state on that since I couldn't explain what was truly scaring me; it would make no sense.

My upline manager sat with me and soothed and calmed me down until she was able to leave me and then I finally fell into the oblivion of drunken sleep.

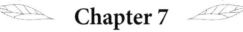

Chapter 7

What On Earth Happened?

Each day the fog of psychosis continued to lift a little and my surroundings slowly came into focus with their clinical reality. The safe and comforting return of saneness conflicted with the bitter reality of a cold hospital bed and the smell of antiseptic. Whilst the psychotic nightmares were fading away they seemed to trade themselves for a new nightmare where I found myself at the mercy of starched nurses and the strict routines of hospital life. I had no choice but to surrender to it, which made me think of "We're Going on a Bear Hunt"— a picture book about all the obstacles a family push through on their expedition to find a bear who is waiting in a cave at the end of the story. The recurring theme is summarised in a repetitive sentence on each page as they encounter each obstacle.

You can't go under it, you can't go over it, oh no! You've got to go THROUGH it.

It's a story of strength and courage as they weave their way through long grass, rivers, forests, and storms. I have such tender memories of sharing this beautiful story with my girls in their early years, and I still quote this sentence to them today when they face difficulties in their life. But now it was my turn to take comfort from it. "I can't go over it, I can't go under it, I've got to go through it."

Another mantra of mine is "nothing is permanent", which are the wise words of my father. He would use them when I was upset at something as a child and, paradoxically, when having a great time on my birthday or at Christmas as an annoying reminder that it would also come to an end. I found myself taking a spoonful of my own medicine, reassuring myself that this would all pass, and my normal life would resume at some point. I just needed to make sure I kept myself topped up with morphine while I waited.

My new periphery was limited, consisting of the white panelled ceiling above me or the grey flip-up cot-sides of my bed, which felt quite claustrophobic at times. I was fed drinks from a straw by turning my head to one side, and at mealtimes, someone tried to feed me, again with me looking awkwardly to the side. The most I could eat in those early days was a single mouthful since apart from having zero appetite, it felt humiliating to be spoon-fed like a baby; little did I know that a Tommy Tippee cup would be coming my way soon.

Now you must appreciate that lying flat on your back unable to move, really is quite a predicament. Apart from my head, my arms were the only part of me that had the freedom to move in the early weeks. At least I could scratch my nose! And, best of all, I could use my mobile phone, and (with practise) write as well. Aware that I needed to find some positivity, my old self-development obsessed brain must have been re-igniting since I started to write in my gratitude book daily. Yes, despite my dire circumstances, I awkwardly held my notebook above me and, using a pencil (since ballpoints are temperamental at writing upside down), would force myself to write three things every day for the entire duration of my recovery. It makes me smile when I read them back today, "saw a white cloud out of the window", "managed to get through the night with less pain", "met a really kind nurse who sat and held my hand". These were the smallest of things that I could find to be grateful for during my new prison sentence.

One of the first necessities brought in by Martin was an extendable backscratcher… a godsend not only for reaching that impossible itch but also for those just out of reach things such as my phone charger lead. It became Martin's new mission; to try to find a resolution to each of my dilemmas with my new constraints as they arose. He found an ingenious green pocket bag from Amazon which fixed via Velcro straps to the cot sides of my bed at shoulder level, enabling me to reach my array of new belongings. It was a bit like one of those organisers you strap to the back of car seats to store colouring books or toys for children's in-car entertainment. The nurses were impressed too, advocating the ward's need for such an ingenious tool as some other patients could also benefit. This bag was soon to become my comfort blanket, my new best friend. It was my lifeline. I would even sleep with my arm resting against it so that I knew it was still there. Oh, how we laughed when we realised that the green tinge to my arm wasn't anything to do with bruising from my blood samples but rather from the dye of the bag. I became weirdly obsessive about it, panicking when the nurses unstrapped it from the bed for my log rolls. It contained all my worldly possessions right now, such as my mobile phone, back scratcher, tissues, a bottle of water, mints (to keep my breath fresh), my glasses and lip balm. My entire life was right there in that one little green bag.

My phone was on my chest a lot of the time so that I knew where it was. It was awkward typing with it up above me and I dropped it on my face many a time (boy, that hurt) until someone kindly brought me one of those button holders to stick on the back of the phone.

Now social media was a welcome companion during my hospital stay, and whilst it was probably a tad early to be back posting on Facebook, it connected me with the outside world which I desperately needed to know was still there; I needed to know that it would wait for me to come back, in whatever shape or form that would be. My business requires me to play an active role on social media, plus I readily admit I'm slightly addicted to the thrill of seeing those little emojis and likes. Despite the haze of psychosis still lingering, I had enough self-awareness to warn myself to tread carefully with my post; I didn't want people to think I was feeling sorry for myself or craving sympathy.

"Just so you all know why I've been a bit quiet. I'm in hospital as I've broken my spine. I'll update you all when I'm a little more comfortable." This post received 181 comments. Wow, my algorithm was going to rocket during my hospital stay! Every cloud…

The one thing I was a bit nervous about was if someone were to ask how it had happened. I needed to make it quite clear from the beginning that this was *not* up for discussion. I would cross that bridge when I came to it, but the first person to ask would get a clear response not just for them but for others as well, that "it wasn't the right time for us to share this information". By us, I meant Martin and myself. We hadn't actually discussed what had happened just five days ago with each other; I guess we were both still in shock. Whilst I was trying to come to terms with the huge battle that lay ahead of me, my head could not compute telling the world what had happened because the truth is, it wasn't very clear to me at that point. Yes, I was aware I had suffered an episode of psychosis but how had I broken my T12 vertebrae? It was lost somewhere in the fog. I reluctantly dragged up the memory to try to make some sense of things...

Enough was enough. When I'd returned from the Tropic event, I had broken down, and told Martin how overwhelmed I was with anxiety. I was terrified of the consequences should the dreaded psychosis word be mentioned, so convinced myself and him this was just a bout of anxiety. But, despite this, on Monday 15 July it was crunch time and, though the deviousness of psychosis was trying to convince me that I was okay, I agreed to go to the doctors with Martin.

I remember sitting in the waiting room at the doctors' surgery unable to make conversation with Martin since my thoughts and feelings were being hijacked now, rendering me tight-lipped and scared. The screen summoned us to the doctor's office. We passed an open door where a patient had collapsed on the floor. The paramedics on the scene were speaking in what seemed especially loud voices; voices I thought were for me.

'Can you hear me?' they said. We walked past but I could still hear them as they gave clear directions. 'We're going to gently lift you up and then carry you out to the ambulance, is that okay?' For some reason, I thought this was a premonition. Their voices were warning me. I had a vision of them coming to collect me, taking me off in a straitjacket to the psychiatric hospital. I took a deep breath, trying to suppress my panic.

As we walked down the long corridor, their voices faded into the distance. We were greeted by a doctor whom I had never met before, which was indicative of our surgery. I was timid and withdrawn, and I was grateful that this doctor would be unaware that this was unusual for me. I started to explain what had been happening, how I was struggling with anxiety and feelings of panic. Martin took over, sensing I was finding it difficult to talk. He emphasised his concern that this could be a sign of another possible "psychotic episode". I nodded my head in agreement, unable to look at him or the doctor.

'And when did you first notice these symptoms, Nicola?' I hated being called this, it made me feel like a child again, like I was in trouble. I found my voice and managed to explain about the BWRT appointment, which was nearly ten days ago now. The doctor seemed very intrigued by this, mostly concerned with the fact I could be suffering some sort of nicotine withdrawal. Martin repeated, more urgently now, about my previous visit to the psychiatric unit, asking for some form of support and questioning whether I needed medication. Why was he making such a fuss? The doctor had just said he thought it was nicotine withdrawal, hadn't he?

As the doctor scanned my notes on the screen, I imagined him thinking the worst of me as he read that I had been admitted to a psychiatric unit for three weeks; did he feel pity for me, or did he think I was crazy? Was he contemplating sending me back there again?

To my surprise, the doctor announced that someone from mental health would get in touch over the next few days and we were sent on our way with some tranquilisers for me to take as and when I felt panicky. What I had been incapable of telling him, and, in fact, Martin, was that I was getting lost inside my head. That whilst I was acting quite calmly on the outside, I had slipped into a deep inner world where I was trapped. Alarm bells were ringing and everything was screaming "Run— something is coming for you, something dark and sinister."

The following night was the night my head truly went BANG. The moment of no return. Lying in bed sometime past midnight, with my eyes wide open, I felt my head shake as if reverberating from a punch from Mohamed Ali. It was accompanied by a loud internal bang.

Initially, just like the last time, I felt calm. The panic had gone, and I experienced a deep blissful peace with a seemingly gifted insight into the whole meaning of life, which I guess sounds a little manic. I still to this day feel it was a genuine moment of enlightenment, but let's not go there. A network of doors and pathways suddenly all opened at once in my head, showing me a world that had been kept hidden in the deepest depths of my mind. It was as if my brain was being pulled apart stitch by stitch, unravelling to reveal things I'd not seen before. It was wondrous, it felt amazing. The universe had miraculously imploded within me. It took my breath away. Time was within me, and, in fact, would stand still for the next seven to ten days.

Psychosis is something very difficult to explain from a place of "saneness", almost as though it has become a foreign language.

When you are in this place of changed reality, thought processes are all very real and significant, building in complexity and all making complete sense at the time. Physically, calmness would switch to panic in an instant, with my body breaking out into a sweat (and not related to my age either). The intense feelings of terror I can only relate to memories of my childhood of waking from a nightmare, out of all perspective and very difficult to put into words. So, fasten your seatbelts and just humour me here as I explain my rollercoaster ride of delusional thoughts.

Now imagine a tiered system of life for just a minute; the ground floor is the world in which you and I live, the sane world that I was now leaving behind. Go up a step to level one, and that is where God and the devil are playing out their story of good and evil through each of us, both of them battling for supremacy (I must add here that I am not a religious person). When I'm on this level, I experience religious beliefs and feel like I've swallowed a bible (this has happened in my previous episodes of psychosis too). Quotes I didn't even know I knew came to me in flashes which I had to scribble down, and during this episode, I became particularly obsessed with the Ten Commandments; I panicked as I couldn't recite all ten, and on Googling them, panicked even more when I discovered that perhaps I'd broken one or two of them which meant being condemned to hell! It was terrifying, and I had flashes through my mind of the "beast", the worst kind of devil, coming for me that night. I believe some people see actual things in front of their eyes (hallucinations) or hear actual voices when experiencing psychosis, but my experience is more like a dream going on inside my head whilst awake.

The next tier, or level two, is above this religious level and is a holding space, or enlightenment. It was one heck of a relief when I arrived here since the religious level was way too scary! It took me back to the blissful calm feelings with a deep inner peace where I would have gladly stayed. However, I was unable to put the handbrake on. Level three was on the top floor, the floor where the Creator, or Director of everything on the other levels resided. I believed that being at this Creator level gave me too much knowledge too fast and feared I may be zapped up into the mothership at any moment. Cool story, but, with my sane mind, I would say most of these delusions are a mixed-up concoction of films including The Matrix (I recall there being an "architect" in Matrix 3 who is reminiscent of my Director).

Now its hardly surprising, with all this going on I didn't get any sleep that night; I was too busy fighting these exhausting battles in my head. My mind continuously jolted me up and down to the different floors of my tiered craziness. Sometimes I was on a clearly-defined level, other times they were merging with each other to further complicate the thought processes. At one point I became stuck at the creator level and this was when my conversations with my dad began; he had already reached this level before me, he had succeeded in finding the secret to life, (something he used to test my thought processes with as a child… I often used to believe that he was God!). The conversation was all in my head (although I may have mumbled out loud). I don't know because Martin was in too deep a sleep to notice.

'You always *were* too clever for your own good, look what you've gone and done now!' my dad said to me, laughing as he told me there would be no going back now that I had worked everything out, and that there would have to be consequences. The night continued with what I truly believed were telepathic conversations with my dad, an exhausting night where he was challenging me with a complex game of mind chess.

As dawn broke and light began to seep in through the bedroom window on what was to be a grey, dull day, BANG, my head jolted again. A new round with Mike Tyson and I was in "purgatory". How had I died and ended up here and not realised? I dragged myself to the bathroom, feeling as though I was caught in some miserable state between life and death and would now be trapped here forever. This was to be my "consequence". I truly believed this. Another film perhaps, this time *What Dreams May Come* with Robin Williams where he has to rescue his wife from hell after she commits suicide. It was to be another of the longest days of my life.

Mental Health called me at some point that day and I was able to say 'yes' in the right places when they informed me that an appointment was being made for twenty-eight days' time and that someone would call me to set a date for that appointment. I said this was fine. How ironic! It would prove to be too little too late…

My head could not differentiate between night and day anymore; I retreated to my bedroom which became my safe space. I was becoming a mere shadow of myself, sinking so deep that I was lost within myself. I didn't feel real; I remember looking in the mirror and not even being able to see my refection. Nikki Rodwell had left the building. What remained was a blurry, rubbed out version of me, soft focused beyond recognition. Life had detached me from its umbilical cord, and I was finding it hard to breathe.

When in the throes of psychosis, my mind can become devious and sharp, alert like a cat in survival mode. I would listen out for Martin and Chloe and dive into the safety of my bathroom if I heard them coming to check on me; hiding myself for fear that if they were in the same room, they may be able to read my thoughts.

Doors become a fixation, along with jewellery. Then there was colour; yes, colours suddenly become significant in my madness too. I started throwing out dozens of clothes whilst rearranging my entire wardrobe. Instead of my usual one wardrobe for winter and one for summer, I felt compelled to mix them all in together to colour code it all to "correctness". Red was thrown out fearing that it would attract the devil, then a whole host of other clothes simply because they had a gold button on (that was evil) or were jinxed by their colour. Everything white had to go too since, heaven help me, yes, I think I believed I was Jesus Christ for a while.

Martin returned from work and came to chat to me in the bedroom while I was mid-wardrobing. I justified my crazy actions by saying I was having a clear out of some clothes. I have asked him since if he thought it was strange how I was frantically throwing items into bin bags for him to take to charity shops; he says not, apparently taking it on face value at the time that I was having a spring clean. Oh, how I wish he had flipping stopped me; I lost a heck of a lot of good clothes and would find myself later in the year wondering where certain tops and designer jackets had mysteriously disappeared to.

A recurring theme in each episode of psychosis is to scribble down lots of erratic notes, almost like rambling reminders of key breakthrough moments in case I should forget them. These notes make interesting reading after the psychosis has passed and are quite haunting.

So, it was Friday 19 July, just three days since seeing the doctor, but it felt more like three years to me. I had been awake all night again living through my "tiered" nightmare and my agitation was starting to worry Martin. He recalls that I would look right through him, with a glazed look that gave him the chills. Both he and Chloe were now clearly noticing my bizarre behaviour and were especially concerned by how I was mumbling to myself, a kind of chatter that was not quite loud enough to catch what I was saying. The doctor had to be called, the doctor who, in my world, was definitely someone to be scared of, someone I could not trust.

Getting no reply, Martin decided to drive down to the surgery and see if he could get some help. I was aware that he was going and as soon as the crunching on the gravel driveway ceased, I rushed to put a few things in my brown leather rucksack, fumbling to put on a zip-up hoody for a hasty exit. I had decided I needed to leave... for good. Martin had now become my enemy and was about to bring me crashing down. The doctor would interrogate me and try to make me crack, revealing that I knew too much, necessitating the need to call people to come and take me away, to lock me up in "that place". I couldn't let it happen. No, my time here was done, there was a new journey ahead of me that I needed to take. I began to feel like I was invincible like Lara Croft at this point, and detached of all emotion for my home, my life, my husband and even my daughter. I set off to escape. *It makes me cry when I read this back.*

Our dogs seemed to be waiting for me at the bottom of the stairs, almost as if they were guarding me. It scared me a little, conjuring up an image of dogs guarding the gates of hell, so I shut them in the lounge and walked out the front door. I didn't want to be seen and was worried I might meet Martin coming back up the road on his return, so I ventured towards our side garden. I looked across the vegetable plot at the fields which stretch for about a mile or so. Depending how quickly he got back he would possibly see me marching there in the distance on his return, so I headed down the garden instead, past the pampas, to the bottom where there was a broken section of wall with a long drop down onto the village hall green. I looked across the green and could see the road where I wanted to get to in the village, but the jump down was too far; I would possibly break my leg or something. In a confused daze I stepped back a bit which was when I noticed a deckchair leaning up against the wall. It was offering itself to me as a ladder to climb up, to escape through the neighbour's garden. I was feeling a sense of urgency now; Martin could be back at any minute.

I clambered through the metal framework of the upturned chair, feeling it sink slightly into the soft ground beneath. With some difficulty I managed to clamber up onto the wall, where, to my horror, it was further down on the other side than I had imagined. Our neighbour's garden was not level with ours.

Heart pounding, I started edging sideways along the wall and managed to get onto the roof of the neighbour's outbuilding; a brick single storey unit with a red-tiled pitched roof. I was almost at the same height as our upstairs landing window; I'd never seen our house from this angle before!

But then it goes hazy, like a mist swirling in from above, my memory fading away with me crouched there on the tiled roof, with my rucksack on my back. I could hear a voice calling to me…

Martin was at my bedside, stroking my hand, and I was almost too embarrassed to look at him. My wonderful kind, loving husband who I knew loved me so much that, despite the craziness of what had happened, he was going to stand by me.

'I fell off the roof, didn't I?'

'No, Nikki,' he said, 'you jumped.'

I had tears streaming down my face.

'It's okay… I'm not going anywhere. We can get through this.'

'I'm so sorry.'

'What for?' He looked puzzled.
'For doing this to us.'
'You didn't do this to us… mental health did this to us.'

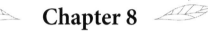

Chapter 8

Changing Opponent

Martin explained to me that I would have to lie flat like this for a minimum of four weeks before they would start to raise me to a sitting position. My spinal cord was in shock apparently and needed a chance to heal. It slowly dawned on me that I going to be here for quite some time. I truly thought they would be kicking me out after a week or two; that I could go home and lick my wounds and start to rebuild my life just like I had when I had returned home from the psychiatric unit before. It hadn't dawned on me that I was here to stay. This cold clinical place was to become my new home for the coming months. Tears started to stream down my face. I just wanted to go home, to be with Martin and my doggies and get back to that normal place, that peaceful, almost blissful life we had.

In the middle of this weepy moment, I had another realisation. Further down the bed, under the sheet, I was aware that I had a catheter in. I could vaguely recall during the chaos in A&E that they had pulled the curtain around and shoved it in quickly. It didn't particularly perturb me though, especially since I had had one after giving birth to Amy, some thirty years before. But what began to dawn on me was, how the heck did you have a poo in this predicament? They wouldn't be allowed to lift me to the toilet, so I was confused about how they would overcome this. I nervously asked Martin what would happen when the "other" end needed to go. He didn't know the answer either, so we asked a nurse, presuming I was to be given a bedpan or something. But no! No such luck. I was lying on a large square puppy training pad for a reason it would seem. I was to release my bowels in the bed! I was horrified in the same way I had been when my mother told me where babies come from; a cruel joke surely? Apparently not; they weren't allowed to move me or lift me onto a bedpan. Spinal patients were too fragile and had their own "special" way of going for a poo. Flat on their back in their own bed.

Now not only was going to the toilet in bed wrong on all levels, but in front of people on the ward? I wouldn't call myself a prude but going to the toilet is an area in my life for which I do expect complete privacy. I mean, even the thought of public toilets makes me break out in a sweat. Of course, there have been times where I have needed that urgent wee, and had no other option, but anything else, I would rather wait and go in the privacy of my own toilet, thank you very much. On the very rare occasions where I have been caught out and had no other option, I have found myself waiting in a cubicle (sometimes for up to half an hour) until the ladies' room has been vacated or for the timely hand dryer to be on before I drop; all because I don't want anyone to hear the splash! Yes, I'm slightly poo phobic, I believe.

Well, as it would turn out, I would have plenty of time to get used to these new toilet arrangements because nothing was going to happen for weeks. Instead, my stomach became increasingly distended, adding stomach pain and queasiness to my list of discomforts. The combination of opioids and lying flat on my back not only gave me no appetite but had also brought my digestive system to a grinding halt.

One of the side effects of my blockage was about to rear its ugly head. My upline manager from Tropic came to visit me with another Tropic colleague and I was mortified when their visit was cut short after I threatened to vomit as I started to feel increasingly poorly. This brought about such panic since I didn't know how I would retch without jarring my back. Apart from anticipating that it would really hurt, I imagined all the intricate metalwork coming apart, ruining the seven-hour operation; it was quite terrifying.

However, I was soon to learn that the body is an amazing thing, not just for the dilemma of vomiting but also other bodily functions like sneezing or coughing. I remember trying so hard to suppress my first sneeze and then the tiniest little "choo" seeped out, saving my body from any movement. A cough would come out as an interrupted kind of throat-clearing sound. It was as if my body cleverly developed its own defence mechanism to protect my back.

Later that evening when the vomit finally made its appearance, nurses were running in all directions with kidney-shaped bowls and it didn't jar my back thankfully. But the colour of the black tar-like stuff that spurted out of me like something from a horror film, was pretty scary. I was immediately put on yet more drugs in the shape of anti-sickness tablets. Thank God they worked quickly.

In my attempts to avoid the discomfort of the present moment and the unnerving interim of not knowing whether my legs would work again or not, I seemed to keep drifting back to thoughts about the roof. I still had this unanswered question in my head, a blank spot. What had made me jump? Although sketchy, I could piece together a lot of my psychotic thoughts, so why couldn't I remember this? It's not like I had sustained a head injury; this had been confirmed by CT scans. No, my back had taken the full blow on a flint stoned wall that separates our neighbours' two gardens. Ouch! I had landed on the gravel in the garden of a neighbour whom I'd never met before. Well, that's one way to introduce yourself, I guess!

As much as I couldn't fully recollect the memory, which was hidden behind a veil, I did recollect a very definite sensation of falling backwards, so how could I have jumped? I didn't feel I could discuss this further with Martin right now, since he was clearly very disturbed by whatever he had seen, and was still trying to process it all. One thing I was certain of though, I had not intended to end my life. My life had never been better, and I had everything to live for. But then again, it hadn't been me up on that roof, had it? My crazed mind may have been escaping some dark monster and forced me to throw myself off. Perhaps I had believed it would get me out of my psychotic nightmare? Maybe I had been so far entrenched that my mind tricked me that I was stuck in a dream and by throwing myself off, I would wake up back in the safety of my bed, like one of those dreams that jolt you awake just before you hit the ground.

I knew it wasn't healthy for my bruised mind to dwell on this any longer, so I left the thought in its holding space for now. I could come back to explore it when the bruise was a little less tender.

Martin and Chloe were very protective of me, especially when it came to guarding the sensitive details surrounding my accident. They managed to handle things tactfully in the outside world; whether it was to protect my fragile ego at the time, or because they were also still trying to get their heads around what had happened. They kept both the psychotic episode and the roof incident securely tucked away, neatly folded in the bottom drawer for now.

On Chloe's first visit after the operation, she was sitting by my bedside filling me in on how Mabel and Chester were missing me when a visitor arrived unannounced and plonked herself down at the end of my bed.

'So, what happened?' she said, just like that. No introductions or warm-up, straight out with it. She was passing by supposedly, so thought she would pop in, obviously to find out what had happened, intrigued by how I had broken my back, wanting the full gossip perhaps. This person wasn't someone involved in my everyday life, not even a friend that I meet for coffee or who has ever been round to my house. She was more of an acquaintance, so I was surprised by her visit.

Chloe was as taken aback as I was and spoke for me. She told her in a curt tone that even I hadn't heard her use before, that we were not discussing it. The awkwardness that followed soon led to the woman leaving. Chloe and I just looked at each other, flabbergasted. I would have to find an easier way to tell people in the future without that tumbleweed moment of awkwardness, but for now, it would have to do. People would just have to respect our privacy.

The problem with this "I'd rather not talk about it" message was how it built the whole thing up into a secret, increasing people's curiosity, which was never the intention. I have since heard from friends how their imaginations ran wild; believing that my boisterous dogs had pulled me over the cliff edge onto the beach, or perhaps Martin and I having had adventurous sex in some Karma Sutra position resulting in my disastrous injury. Wow, that conjures up an image. It does make me laugh though and probably would have been easier to explain.

So, you may be asking yourself, why didn't we say something simple, make something up? Why not just say I slipped off a roof? Well, then obviously people would ask what on earth I was doing up on a roof. What would I say then? Rescuing a cat? Fixing a missing tile maybe? No, in my experience, if you start lying, you're then forced to elaborate with more lies, ending in a whole web of untruths to get tangled up in. Plus, the very heart of me hates dishonesty anyway, so it wasn't an option. Then another thought started to niggle away at me. What if the rumour got out that I had jumped from a roof leading people to form their own conclusion that I had tried to commit suicide? All it would take was one person to mention the roof and surely Chinese whispers would run wild with everyone questioning why I had wanted to end my life. If you didn't know about the psychotic episode it would be a natural assumption to make, wouldn't it?

I couldn't bear the thought. I would most definitely have to find a way to explain, a tactful and comfortable sentence that would sum it all up nicely.

It was sometime towards the end of the first week that I became aware of a presence by the side of my bed. I had a nurse sitting next to me day and night, watching over me. There was no announcement of her arrival, just like the subtle changeover of seasons, no defining moment of where or when she had begun. I presumed she was there because of the nature of my injury and how serious it was, to check that I wasn't moved or handled in the wrong way. The NHS had kindly given me a full-time assistant which was very handy because she would fetch the meds nurse for me when my pain became unbearable or top up my water if needed; even be there to hold my hand when I felt like crying. Hah! As if. No, with the pressures of NHS staffing, to indulge in such a luxury for every back-injury patient would be ludicrous. It wasn't so much because of my "special" injury that she was there but (unbeknownst to me) because of a recommendation by the mental health team to make sure I didn't try to harm myself or attempt to get out of bed. It seemed they may have heard the Chinese whisper and believed I was a danger to myself which, thankfully, was something I was oblivious to until much further down the line, as was Martin. Each "bedside assistant" was discreet, changing shifts without my even noticing, and slipping out of sight when I had visitors.

Before the end of my first week, Chloe visited again with Martin, and they both showed up with a surprise guest. Amy. She had dropped everything and flown down from Scotland to come and visit me. It was lovely to see her and she seemed particularly loving. Oh god, I hoped she didn't think this had all happened because of her ignoring my birthday or her harsh messages? I hoped she didn't have any guilt. It crossed my mind, but I couldn't say anything, I couldn't find the words.

As I was still very drugged up and at the tail end of psychosis, the conversation wasn't very forthcoming. I smiled and thanked her for coming and reassured her that I was okay.

'I'm here for you, Mum.' She leant over and hugged me before leaving. She was staying at home with Martin and Chloe and would be coming back to see me the next day. However, this soon changed. I received a message from her that evening and couldn't believe what I read.

'What's this? Why would you say I have a venomous tongue? It's Steph who has the venomous tongue, not me.' Along with this text was a photo of something written by me in very strange and shaky writing. I enlarged it on my small iPhone screen, and it took a few minutes for me to absorb. It seemed she had found some of my psychotic ramblings on my office desk. She had opened a notebook and found a page where amongst other crazy things such as "religious jargon", I had written "venomous tongue" with the name "Amy" written close by. My heart started to speed up with stress and confusion. I started wracking my brain, trying to remember what else I may have written.

Now it may well be intrusive to read someone's personal diary, but the ramblings of my psychotic brain were a step too far. I felt a mixture of devastation but also anger so I didn't reply, for fear of saying the wrong thing. But then I started getting angry messages pouring in, and, becoming overwhelmed, I messaged Martin, who I knew would rescue me from this. She should never have read it, and she clearly needed to have it explained to her that a person in a psychotic state should not be held accountable for something they were probably totally unaware they were even doing. Martin was there at home with her, so I begged him to tell her to stop, forwarding him some of the messages I was receiving.

Unfortunately, Martin lost the plot with her, not only for snooping in my office but also for messaging me when I was so vulnerable. He kicked her out, accusing her of "making it all about her", telling her that she was selfish to be adding to my stress. She was sent packing back to Scotland, and that was the last I saw of her. Wow, I hadn't seen that coming but then I guess emotions were running high and Martin had the new role of protecting me whilst I was still so vulnerable.

The whole Amy thing was upsetting, but my survival instinct told me to put it away and not overthink it. I knew it would be some time before she and I would talk again, but for now, that had to be okay. My focus had to be on learning to adapt to my new predicament. My mental health battle was nearly over, but for the first time in my life, I needed to find the strength to fight for my physical wellbeing.

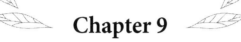

Chapter 9

Despicable Me

The first week of my hospital sentence passed and the psychosis had lifted— Nikki Rodwell was back in the room! I evolved back to the chatty, friendly, effervescent person that I am. Well, maybe I wasn't quite fizzing over. I wasn't exactly having a party, and a selfie I took at the time reminds me of just how poorly I was; a deathly grey pallor, sunken eyes underlined with dark shadows, looking like I'd just been to hell and back. Well, I had! However, despite the torturous psychological nightmare I had been through and the initial wave of physical pain, things were becoming much more comfortable.

Some of the nurses who had seen me when I had first arrived must have thought of me like Jekyll and Hyde, changing from the silent, mistrusting person I had been in psychosis to this new more alert and brighter person.

One of the positive things I started doing was visualisation. Well, there wasn't a lot else I could do flat on my back. I had practised it a little with my self-development routines, but nothing compared to what I was about to embark on.

My friend Julie came to visit when she heard of my predicament, to work some holistic magic on me with a bit of reflexology. I think she may have done some reiki too but am unsure since I was comatose in a complete state of bliss for most of her visit! We had a long chat when she first arrived, and I found myself opening up to her about my experience and confiding in her what had happened. I knew she was someone who would understand since she had been through a similar mental health episode herself; I guess this made it feel safe to tentatively talk about it for the first time. It was so comforting to share with someone who had experienced something similar. The reflexology brought immediate relief to my body but equally, my soul was massaged; feeling accepted, understood, and loved as a human being.

Julie also happens to be very knowledgeable about hypnotherapy and was concerned by what I described of my BWRT experience. She confirmed what I had been thinking; that I had been hypnotized. The flickering eyes indicated REM (rapid eye movement) which is experienced when a person is in a hypnotic state. It made me feel sick to think that an innocent appointment to give up nicotine could have resulted in this.

As soon as Julie left the ward, I googled in search of any correlation between hypnosis and psychosis, and whilst quite weak, there *is* some significance. I rushed to message Martin and Chloe to share what I'd learnt, but they didn't seem as disturbed by the information as I did. It had felt like a moment of enlightenment to me, the explanation I needed as to what had possibly triggered the psychosis. But maybe they felt I was looking for someone to blame? I wasn't. I was just trying to make head or tail of where it had all begun; I'm the sort of person who likes to work things out, to make sense of it all. My mind wanted to tidy up the beginning and the ending of my psychotic episode.

Julie and I had talked about the power of visualisation at the end of her visit, with her strongly encouraging me to give it a go. She explained how I could have a direct impact on my physical recovery with my mental input. Kind of mind over matter. Well, that seemed ironic since the mental input had most definitely put me in this predicament in the first place! But I was prepared to do anything that might give me a better chance of walking again, even if it did seem a bit hocus pocus, so I decided I had nothing to lose by practising it and possibly everything to gain.

I'm an all or nothing kind of person and this was to be no exception to the rule. Firstly, I did some research. There seemed to be lots of scientific data with positive results confirming my decision to give this my best shot. I decided to start with the most pressing of matters, which was to get my bowels going again. I wanted to go home with my bowel and bladder intact more than anything else in the world... possibly even more than walking. Interesting that I gave myself the luxury of believing I could choose one over the other; disabled in a wheelchair, or incontinence. Little did I know that most SCI patients live with *both*. Well, I'd never really thought about it before, just like I'd never thought about toilet issues from a hospital bed.

So back to my visualisation... I knew that instead of *fearing* incontinence, I had to start visualising the opposite. To picture myself sitting on the white ceramic toilet in our compact ensuite at home, whilst taking in the beautiful view from the side window.

I'd never even seen the film *Despicable Me* so I have no idea why I chose the little yellow minions to be the workers in my visualisation; hundreds of them at different points from my stomach down to my bowel, through to rectum, anus and finally sphincter. I pictured the bright yellow little men dressed in their blue dungarees with a miner's light fixed on their head over their eye.

While it might sound like I'm losing the plot, my mind had never been clearer; desperate times needed desperate measures. I would close my eyes, rub my stomach, and talk to my minions (not out loud obviously!) willing them to help me. I imagined numerous railway crossings complete with barriers and lights, but the gates were faulty and unable to lower to allow the safe passage of a train. I asked my minions to locate the appropriate emergency service to fix the barriers along the line so that normal service could resume.

There were also minions in their gym attire working out a little further up the track, re-teaching the upper muscles of my stomach the art of peristalsis, pushing everything down from the top end through the stomach. I made the picture as vivid and as crazy as I could and believed they would feel my thoughts and hear my instructions; they were my allies, here to help in my battle on the road to recovery.

I later employed lady minions into my bladder to sort out all my wee issues and ensure that I got full function back after catheter removal. I made up an image of female minions in cute little dresses with aprons on, wearing nurses' hats with a red cross on, just like the one I had with my nurse's outfit as a little girl. I had no idea if female minions even existed having not seen the films; I had only ever seen pictures of their yellow husbands in blue dungarees and miners' hats!

All my little blue-collar workers were set to work; wives at the front and husbands at the back, separated from each other until their jobs were done! I was a little blown away when I later discovered that not only do female minions exist, but they look very much like the picture I had conjured up in my mind, complete with little white hats adorned with red crosses. It may all seem a little unbelievable, but I really had nothing to lose and everything to gain.

I started to practise this visualisation for around twenty minutes a day, sometimes longer. Oh, how Martin laughed when I told him. He did think it was brilliant and I knew like always, that he totally believed in me and was proud of my progress. He did have to add his two-pennies' worth though, encouraging me to add further visualisations of walking... as if I needed to be reminded of the need to walk again! I made it the last thing I pictured in my mind as I drifted off to sleep each night; walking on the beach feeling the sand between my toes, or looking down at my muddy muck boots as I walked through the woods with my doggies, putting one foot in front of the other.

I do feel that all hospitals should have some sort of counselling service for people with specific injuries that are going to require them to have bowel care, because the experience is quite shocking, probably not the same for everyone, but something I most definitely wasn't prepared for, and could not discuss or talk about even with close friends. It has left a lasting memory firmly imprinted in my mind.

The words bowel care conjure up an image of a doctor asking you lots of questions and generally caring about your bowels. The truth is very different. With four nurses carefully rolling me on my side, one lucky nurse got to poke an enema in the form of two pessaries up my back passage to see if it would trigger a bowel movement. Each time they came back to check if anything had happened it never had, and I felt like a disappointment, a waste of their time. I would then have to endure a rectal examination and a sweep of my bowel with a nurse's finger rudely inserted high up my rectum to see if anything was up there. It was uncomfortable and painfully embarrassing. This continued daily along with doses of laxatives and stool softeners, but to no avail. The top end of my bowel was impacted, and nothing seemed to be moving down. This caused an increasing sense of panic as the days passed by and I began to imagine that my distended stomach might burst and explode my poop around the entire ward. I would check in with Martin daily to give him updates, desperate to give him the news that something had finally happened. But my stomach continued to grow larger and larger. There was no sign of "the train" coming down the track and the pain in my abdomen just increased. I started to have very firm conversations with my minions, threatening redundancies if they didn't get their "shit" together.

Martin was very anxious about getting to visit me as soon as he could get away from the café. The poor man was being torn in half. The timing of my hospitalisation couldn't have been any worse…

The café had been my idea. I had always known Martin wanted to run a café, something he never thought would be possible, a pipe dream. It's not that he complained about being a painter and decorator with his one-man-band decorating business, just his radio for company day in and day out. But in recent years it had started to make me sad to see how mundane his work had become for him; I know I couldn't do a job as boring as watching

paint dry. It seemed almost criminal that such a large vivacious man was confined to people's empty homes, paintbrush in hand. 'He's wasted,' his mother would say. 'He could have been the next Michael Ball.' But he never grumbled since it allowed him the time to carry out his hobby in life; amateur dramatics.

But I felt guilty. I was living it up with my direct sales business, winning top sales awards and working my way up through Tropic's compensation plan. There were constant girls' prosecco weekends away, spa days, meals out, and then the Glammies— the big bi-annual event shared with ambassadors from all around the country to celebrate our successes and watch the launching of new products with motivational talks by Lord Sugar (who is co-owner of the company) and Susie Ma, the founder and creator of Tropic. A load of excited women all glammed up and having one big party was hardly work, more of a piss-up really. This, and other fun nights away, was all part of the business and something which Martin fully supported, always being left behind to look after our dogs since spouses were not invited.

So, it dawned on me that the remnants of my cash from the sale of our last house, just sitting in the bank earning no interest, could be used to surprise him with a café, if one came up at the right price. Well, about a year later, that *one* just happened to turn up in Cromer, the next seaside town along from us, and we went to check it out and meet the owners. It was larger than the café I had envisaged, not your quaint afternoon-tea type of place (which would have been more Margo's cup of tea!), but more your belly-busting, good old English breakfast and builder's tea type of place. Martin wanted to go for it so that's what we did.

There were some complications with our initial offer, and we were nearly "gazumped" until our prospective landlady stepped in to help us out. She had the final say and advised the sellers of the café to go with us as she had known Martin for some years and didn't like the sound of the other purchaser. There was still one problem though, we were short by around £20K toward the purchase price and we would need extra to pay for initial supplies and other expenses in our first month. We had shared this information with our landlady and explained that we just needed some time to source where we would raise the extra money.

Martin and I were having a drink and a bite to eat in the Red Lion whilst mulling over how we could raise this extra cash, when a rainbow appeared through the window in front of us, overlooking the sea. I simply love rainbows and told Martin that it was a sign, and I was right. By mere fluke, our fairy godmother breezed in (our landlady) and offered to loan us the extra cash to help get us going. Just like that, £20K interest free! I was completely taken aback by her generosity and kindness and sat in stunned silence whilst she joined us for a drink. I knew Martin had known her for some years, but I'd only met her a handful of times. I truly believe it may be a Norfolk thing, as you would never find such trusting and generous types down in Surrey where I used to live. I am indebted to her not just for her loan, but her support and trust in both of us.

We set up a partnership and completed on the contract at the end of April 2019; Breakers became our café and Martin's dream opened up in front of him. It was never my intention to get very involved since I had my own business to manage, and another trip to win, but then I had never imagined myself being laid up in hospital and quite *this* idle in my support! Martin, on the other hand, hit the ground running with our fifty-seater hustling and bustling café. He was learning the ropes, managing staff rotas, stock supplies and sorting out suppliers during the busiest season of the year. It should have been a happy time for him, but I think the shock of managing this new venture whilst having me in a hospital some forty-five minutes away must have overstretched him beyond belief. It was going to continue for quite some time too…

I knew when he was approaching the ward as there would be a faint commotion out in the corridor and the sound of nurses laughing as he chatted and joked on his way in. He would breeze into the room, larger than life, chatting with familiar faces on the ward who seemed as pleased to see him as I was! He would come laden with gifts for me, mostly food which I would turn away and he would happily sit and eat for me. He brought in Tropic toiletries that I needed, magazines, mints, notebooks and pens. He would patiently spend the first ten minutes sorting my green bag for me, making sure I knew what was in each pocket before he left. He was kind and loving, albeit a tad overpowering at times, but that is just his enthusiasm to fix things for me and try to protect me.

I, however, was perfectly despicable in those early weeks. I am embarrassed to admit that I was constantly complaining in true "Margo" style, insisting that I wanted to go private when I couldn't cope with things like being missed for my morning bed bath, or not having my buzzer responded to. Whilst my smiles and positivity were portrayed to the nurses and my daily visitors from Mental Health, poor Martin got the brunt of my frustrations, fears, and impatience. His background of some twenty odd years working in care as a residential social worker stood him in good stead, and prepared him to deal with this irritable, complaining, and demanding wife that I had become.

'What do you mean you've forgotten them?' I snapped. There were two things I desperately needed and had ordered from Amazon; some padded headphones to block out the sounds of the ward and an eye mask to block out the bright lights. I snapped his head off when he explained he had forgotten to pick them up in his rush to get over to see me.

Something had been worrying me and I'd been waiting to talk to him about it, so I changed the subject. Despite knowing I was out the other side of my psychosis I still felt there may be some consequences, possibly having to go back to that awful place. I hardly dared to ask him but needed to know.

'No, hun, you won't be going to a psychiatric unit again, Mental Health are putting some support in place for you... but from here you will be going direct to Sheffield to focus on your recovery and learn to walk again.' Sheffield. Sherry the spinal nurse had told me about this place. She would sweep in most days to check in on me and discuss my injury, bowels, or catheter issues. She had told me that Sheffield was a specialist unit which provided intense therapy for people with spinal injuries like mine, a kind of boot camp that would get you mobile and functioning again. But there was a waiting list, and nobody seemed to know how long it might take.

'I don't want to go to Sheffield,' I said, giving Martin my best sulky child look. I just wanted to go home; the thought of travelling up north to another strange hospital, 150 miles away from him and my home terrified me. Surely I didn't have to go if I didn't want to? No, I would refuse.

'Nikki, I don't think you're understanding the nature of your injury; you've damaged your *spinal* cord, do you understand what that means?'

'Of course, I know what that fucking means...' I snapped, glaring at him. But the truth is I didn't. And I didn't want to. Somewhere in the back of my mind I thought the spinal cord was something to do with the central nervous system, and that sounded too scary to contemplate. I didn't want to talk about it so I cut the conversation dead. I had broken my T12 vertebrae and the operation I had had would fix that; I didn't need to understand any more than that right now.

Poor Martin would have to put up with my despicable attitude on most of his visits, in addition to coping with a bombardment of whingey messages. It seemed that the longer my awaited poo took to come, the shittier I seemed to become, as if the toxic poison inside was seeping outward through my very being.

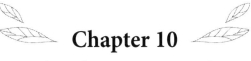

Chapter 10

The Other Man in My Life

I was so relieved when I was introduced to my physio routine, albeit a snatched twenty minutes from an overstretched physio team in their busy schedule. It meant I was on my way, moving in the right direction towards repairing myself. The ladies who came to do my leg exercises and stretches were like angels, always smiling, gentle and kind, answering my endless questions with such patience. They even looked like angels too, with their perfect blonde hair neatly tied back, glowing skin and perfect smiles, wearing their crisp white tunics.

In my first session, I realised that getting back on my feet was not going to be an overnight thing. Vicky held my legs and made cycling movements, gently mobilising my feet, ankles and legs. It felt wonderful, as if they were gently being woken up from a deep sleep, although she couldn't bend my knee too far since the backs of my legs were painfully tight. Vicky was impressed by how much I could move my feet and toes, and there was a fair amount of movement in my right leg too. The left leg had far less potential, but I needed to focus on the positive, that at least it had some movement. She refused to confirm whether or not I would be able to walk again; she just gave me a reassuring smile each time I asked her. I guess in hindsight they had to be careful not to build my hopes up.

Now I'm not the most patient of people at the best of times, and I was determined to fast-track as much as I could here. I believed if I could do double the number of exercises suggested by physio, I'd give myself a better chance of walking sooner and get home to my doggies that I missed so much. I would do my homework. I would set goals— something I knew I was good at, something that may just give me back the little bit of control that I needed. I would continue with the new method of achieving success that I had discovered before this accident had so rudely interrupted my progress.

It was back in May, shortly after we had invested in the café, that I discovered another man who would play a very large part in my life. It was due to my endless quest for personal growth that I stumbled across Hal Elrod, a coaching guru from the United States who has experienced great adversity in his life; lessons he now shares with millions of people. I think we all find someone in life who really speaks to us at one point or another, the influence of a family member, teacher from school, or a wise friend who gives us some profound words of wisdom and support when we are at a crossroads in our life, someone we admire and would perhaps like to emulate.

I can't remember how I stumbled across Hal's book "The Miracle Morning" but it came just at the right time for me since I needed to reboot my Tropic business a little. It was just the right motivation for me to up my game; I needed to increase my personal sales and bring some new people into my team if I wanted to win that year's trip.

Now, these trips are hard to achieve but so worth it. Back in January I had been on an all-expenses paid trip to South Africa which I didn't think could possibly top the previous year's trip to Mauritius. But it did. Tropic pulled out all the stops and truly made it a trip to remember. We stayed in the most prestigious hotel in Sun City and they put on an extravaganza of galas, parties and firework displays by night and then, of course, safari excursions by day where I got to witness the Big Five! I hadn't even known this should have been on my bucket list, that I would be so enchanted with the true beauty of seeing animals in their natural habitat. It was simply amazing, and to share this mini trip with two hundred other excited Tropic ambassadors made it an experience never to be forgotten. This year was a trip to Cambodia & Vietnam, another area of the world I had never experienced, and there was no way I was missing out on it.

"The Miracle Morning" set me the new challenge of discovering my true potential and increasing my chances of success by getting up an hour earlier every morning to do a set of rituals. These included meditation, visualisation, affirmations, yoga and exercise. Now I love learning new things, but for me to attempt getting up at 6.00 a.m., this was no mean feat. Martin always says I'm not a morning person, with a capital N. In fact, he will drop me a cup of tea on my bedside table and RUN before I open my eyes, fearful of the bleary-eyed cavewoman that emerges in the morning. I've always been the kind of person who hits repeat on the snooze button for as long as possible, and as I work from home, this can be quite perilous. It would take my impatient dogs to start licking my face and whimpering for me to let them out somewhere between eight and 9.00 a.m. to finally get me to decamp from my snuggle place. So, it was indeed quite some miracle in the making when I started to successfully get up at six every morning.

After finding myself an accountability partner, I set my alarm clock for 6.00 a.m. (across the other side of our bedroom so I would have to get out of bed to reach it) and started the day, to see if the "magic" would work on me. The book claimed that a dedicated first hour of focusing on mindset would then have a knock-on effect for the following hour, setting the scene for a successful morning and the remainder of the day. What did I have to lose? I tapped into Hal Elrod's podcasts and blogs and became more and more inspired by this American guy. He had done his research and it seemed all successful people in life are early risers and engage in these sorts of early rituals.

I continued bouncing out of bed to my 6 a.m. alarm for the full thirty-day challenge, and I don't quite know how, but things started to happen. By the middle of June, quite a few new ladies had joined my team, and they were great; they took to the business like ducks to water. My team was growing, my sales were increasing, and my business was thriving again. I had successfully changed my record from "I'm *not* a morning person" to "I *am* a morning person."

I loved the person I had become. I loved my business. I loved my husband and the life we had with our dogs. I was proud of how I was truly winning. But then some would say pride comes before a fall…

The stirring of the ward at 6.30 a.m. was in stark contrast to my home life. No birdsong to be heard, no comfy bed or two doggies licking my hand to gently wake me up to my idyllic surroundings. My day used to start with me padding across our carpet to our little ensuite for my first wee of the day, to sit there and look out of the window to assess the weather by the colour and movement of the corn in the beautiful rolling fields. No, instead there was the faint clatter of the tea trolley making its way up the corridor and the bustle of nurses all getting ready for the morning shift changeover. The bright cold lights were an unfriendly alarm clock beginning the day in my new clinical home. I would move my feet first, feeling the stiff white sheet and padded blocks propping them up to prevent foot drop. Yes, of course, I googled it! Keeping the foot angled up would hopefully compensate for the temporary paralysis in the muscles holding my feet up. I figured this was especially important for my left foot which was still refusing to lift up and down. I was allowed a slight tilt on my bed now so long as there was no bend or kink in the middle and my back remained perfectly flat. This slight incline would cause me to slip down on the plastic mattress, so the blocks were also handy for keeping me in position further up the bed.

God, I felt homesick, especially first thing in the morning and last thing at night. I wanted to get home so badly. I yearned for Martin's goodnight kiss; I missed his hugs and even his snoring. My doggies would be missing me by now and I hated the thought that they might think I was gone for good. Whilst I know dogs probably don't think like this, Mabel *had* apparently taken my pyjamas off the bed and dragged them down to her basket where she was lying with them as her comfort blanket. She was definitely missing me!

I decided the best chance I could give myself to get home to my little family sooner rather than later was to re-start my previous discipline of the miracle morning, albeit a slightly adapted version. I would intentionally wake around 6.00 a.m. before other patients had stirred and start by doing ten minutes of visualisation followed by leg exercises. My Jane Fonda padded hand weights were fuchsia pink and black with little Velcro straps for the knuckles. These were to help me to get ahead of the game and make sure I was gaining some strength in my upper body. Well, in the event that I may have to use a wheelchair, I was going to make sure I had some strength to wheel the damn thing. The longer you are laid flat, the more your core muscles wither away. Google told me that for every week of flat bed rest, muscles take one month to recover. How could that be possible?

Social media was already becoming an outlet that helped me forge ahead and face each day; a place where I could be cheered on and supported by friends and family. They loved being involved in my near-daily updates and dilemmas, sometimes making suggestions for great music tracks to listen to or books to read. Well, now they were about to become my accountability partner. I knew that if you write your goals down you are far more likely to achieve them, but was now about to learn that if you write them down on social media, this increases two-fold. So it was, on 1st August, I put a post on Facebook telling everyone that I would take twenty steps by the end of August. I had said it, so I would make it happen, somehow. In all honesty, I had no idea what I was doing. Nobody had given me any idea of timelines, but I believed a month gave me a realistic amount of time. I had no doubt in my mind that I *would* take steps at some point and I had to start somewhere. I would have been in here for six weeks by then, so surely it would be about time to be going home?

I set about designing a page in my shiny new notebook with a list of foot and leg exercises to do. The columns represented Monday to Sunday and the rows a list of exercises for left and right leg. I even managed to rule lines upside down; I was becoming quite dexterous with horizontal life now. The exercises may sound simple: ankle circles, flexing my knee to slide my leg a little and turning my leg inwards and outwards, but I set myself high repetitions which were exhausting. I believed these small movements were all positive signs of a good recovery, albeit the left leg still had some catching up to do. This was confirmed by Mr Lomjay when he checked in on me one day,

'Yes, Nicola, I think this is the best result we could have hoped for. These movements definitely lend themselves to the possibility that you may get the strength to walk.'

Martin sat there, tears streaming down his face when he heard this. I just smiled. Well, of course I was going to walk again. I don't think I ever believed otherwise, and, in fact, I complained when I was given a booklet from a charitable organisation called the Spinal Injury Association as it showed every person in a wheelchair and no walkers. I had googled a little about my injury and there were most definitely cases of SCI people who could walk, and I was going to be one of them. I was furious that the booklet didn't encompass this positivity and decided I would have to do something about it when I got out of there!

It took a lot of willpower to start each day, believe me. I could have just laid there and dozed until the breakfast trolley arrived, spending the day feeling sorry for myself, wondering why I had been struck with the psychotic episode, depressed that it had led to this broken back. No, it was by no means easy. I had to fight through such negativity, and this is where music became of huge significance for me. I would put on my favourite rock tracks and start my morning bed aerobics to "All Right Now" by Free, whilst other patients were still asleep. I was oblivious to the outside world as the music pumped through my veins, even to the handover staff who all lined up at the end of my bed, clipboards in hand, to discuss my injury. As they stood there giving an update on my bowels, (or rather lack of), and my other medical details (such as my low blood pressure) I would smile at them as I continued working out to the sounds of AC/DC. It must have been a funny sight, to see this woman with a broken back lying there with pink pastel headphones on, pushing pink and black hand weights up and down like she was in a private gym.

Breakfast was brought around 8.00 a.m. in the form of soggy Weetabix or chewy toast. I would tend to go for the toast option since I was dairy-free, and they didn't have anything exotic like "alternative" milk to have with cereal. I was labelled what they called a "red tray". My food would arrive on a red tray (funny that!) and would be dumped on a trolley-table to the side of my bed just out of reach, letting me watch my chewy toast go cold. The fact that the tray was red signalled to the nursing staff that a patient needed to be helped with their food, and if you were lucky a nurse would arrive to help feed you before it got snatched back by the catering staff. I soon learnt that if the catering staff angled the table in a certain way as they dumped the plate down, I could manage to feed myself, learning a technique without dropping it all around my neck too. Little moments of independence like this were great breakthroughs.

After breakfast, depending on who was on duty, I would get brought a bowl of warm water and given my toiletries so that I could wash myself, followed up with nurses washing the parts I couldn't reach and changing my bedding. That was on a good day. On a bad day such as a weekend, when invariably there would be agency staff on, it could be as late as 2.00 p.m., causing "Margo" to kick off again and send a complaint to the helpline at martin.com!

I felt like a human being again after my ABC morning routine. This was my Tropic cleanse, tone and moisturise which I could do myself. I would plop the bamboo cloth over my face to steam my pores open and inhale the eucalyptus oil. Never had I appreciated the uplifting aroma so much; it filled my whole body with comfort and reassurance. As I closed my eyes, the revitalizing smell took me away from this world of white ceilings and bed rolls and back to my little bathroom with its white sink and cracked vanity mirror. Yes, this daily luxury grounded me, brought me to a place of calm and comfort from behind my closed curtain and reminded me of home.

After my facial, it was time to wash my body and, as time progressed, I could remove my gown without assistance. With my flimsy curtains drawn around me like the walls of an imaginary bedroom, and using my Tropic body wash, I would gently clean the top half of my body. Wow, more independence. It is hard to explain, but it was as if my back and the bed had fused into one; there was no instinct or ability to move my back off the bed which may have been the body's way to protect itself but also perhaps, due to lack of core muscles. So, leaning forward was not an option and, as the back of the bed wasn't raised yet, my thighs were as far as I could reach, so the nurses would then come and finish me off, washing my legs and feet. I particularly loved having my feet washed as the strange pins and needles sensations I had in them were soothed by the warm water and the touch of human hands massaging them. This time of pampering was the closest I would come in a long time to the luxury of soaking in a warm bath, a treat I used to love to indulge in.

Next came the fun game of my nurse trying to round up three other nurses for a log roll to clean my back before dressing me and changing my sheets. One would arrive, maybe two, then the original nurse would go off to find the third who would arrive but now we'd lost the original. They would to and fro like an episode of Keystone Cops until finally we had the correct number to safely log roll me.

After my backwash and my not-so-subtle sales pitch to convince the girls that they really should buy some Tropic body wash from me, I was dressed in new surgical socks and a fresh gown. The bedding was pulled from beneath me, like a magician pulling a tablecloth out without disturbing the crockery and then I was rolled down on to a fresh sheet with a slide sheet underneath me. This was a sheet with handles so that four nurses could slide me back up the bed if I had slipped down. I hated it and would beg them to slide me slowly since I felt vulnerable, like the top of my head was going to hit the headboard when they whisked me up.

This freshen up and change of gown was so important to set me up for the day; it was crucial to make me feel a little bit like the old me. I felt revitalised in the way you feel after a shower at the gym, although I dearly wished someone would wash my hair! It was looking like an oil slick after three weeks. I asked, but of course, there was never anybody who had a spare five minutes to do this.

Visiting hours were from 1.30 p.m. and the day after I began my Miracle Morning routine, which seemed an uncanny coincidence, my upline leader came to visit me.

"Hi, boss," I said when I saw her approaching. I was cringing a little inside, almost embarrassed by my predicament and her seeing me like this. I call her boss, but the reality is we are all equals in Tropic. I remember her looking down on me (well, everyone seemed to be these days) and kissing me, being her usual cheery and kind self.

'Looks like you're going to win the trip, Nikki… you're nearly there with your points.' What? The Cambodia trip? I'd nearly forgotten all about it. The work I had put in was still paying its dividends. The cogs were still turning outside of this hospital and my points were now standing at around 34,000 apparently, with nearly a month to go.

I decided I had to do something pro-active since it would be disastrous should I fall just short of the 40,000 points

I needed. So, I set about contacting my customer group on Facebook, setting up something called an E-pamper whereby they order from my online shop and the items go into a basket for a large pamper order managed by me. I offered everyone the option of direct delivery which they would have to pay for or collection from Martin at the café. The sales started to come in! It felt great. I was regaining a little more control of some normality and my old life; I had another goal to aim for. Thank you, Hal!

Whilst settling into hospital life, adapting to my new routine and striving to regain some positivity, poor Martin continued to get the darker moments and the wrath of my frustrations. The difficulties imposed on me on a daily basis were unbearable at times and he was my only outlet. Being flat on my back seemed to make me feel extremely vulnerable, which in turn made me feel nervous to complain. Subconsciously I felt that if I upset any of the nurses by complaining, they might leave me until last for my morning wash or maybe ignore my buzzer to come and help me. They might be a little rougher with me when rolling or washing me. Totally irrational probably, but I was 100 per cent reliant on them. There *were* a couple of nurses that scared me too, a bit like that stern sports teacher at school who could kill you with their death stare for no apparent reason. I think it was the starkness of my clinical home and the fact that my carers wore uniform that brought a sense of discipline which rendered me incapable of standing up for myself (which is very unlike me) and made my dependence on Martin even greater.

A heated debate ensued on Martin's next visit. I asked if he had seen my Facebook post stating my intention to take twenty steps by the end of the month. He gave me a disapproving look and told me that he was a believer in keeping goals realistic and that I shouldn't set them too high for fear of being let down. I argued that if you don't aim high, you don't work hard enough and reach your maximum potential. Martin doesn't even like goals, he is much more laid back than me and has a *mañana* attitude which drives me crazy. He and I are very different in this respect. The heated debate developed into a full-on argument with us trying to keep our voices down to spare the others on the ward.

'Oh, just fuck off, it's clear we're completely incompatible.' Despite knowing how badly he reacts to being told to "fuck off", I spat the words at him and pointed for him to leave. Surely it was better to be setting goals rather than lying here and just giving up? Why wasn't he encouraging me to go for it?

After he left, I decided I would write to my pal Hal. Hal Elrod would understand my need to set my goals high. I could tell him about my amazing results from the Miracle Morning so far; how my team were doing so well and that it was looking like I would win the trip thanks to him. I also wanted him to know how I wound up in hospital with the prospect of not walking again, just like he had! In "The Miracle Morning", he touches on his experience of how he ended up in hospital in his early twenties, with eleven broken bones and some brain damage after a head-on collision with a lorry. He defied all the odds and walked out of that hospital six weeks later, having been told he might not walk again. I felt the similarity of our experiences gave me a deeper connection to him. I guess I was reaching out for some kind of inspiration at this point in my journey; I needed some guidance for my next step.

I set about composing an email to him and decided to download his first book to my kindle, which was neatly placed in the second pocket, bottom right of my beloved green bag. But would he actually reply? Hal is very big in America, a motivational speaker, and much sought-after guest for podcasts and large conventions. He is also the author of four bestselling books and master of his own podcast "Achieve Your Goals". I very much doubted he would have time to respond to fan mail from someone like me.

Poor Martin stopped off at the hospital chapel after he left, probably to say a little prayer. He would often do this, almost to bridge the gap between his visits and return journey with a little moment of calm. I can see now, that whilst I threw myself into setting goals trying to take back some control, it also had the benefit of being a distraction. It meant I didn't have to think about how I would face the world and tell them about my psychotic episode, and also it distracted me from how I wasn't coping. The "Margo" in me could be so standoffish and stressed, the child in me could easily burst into tears just because I didn't want another needle in my arm, the teenager in me would sulk if I felt I was being ignored… I was far from winning. Whilst I had found empowerment after I first moved to Norfolk all those years ago, it was because I *chose* to change; it had been *my* decision to up my game and shift my attitude. The difference here, was that this change had come out of the blue, giving me no choice in the matter. My new enforced set of circumstances was a dramatic change like I had never experienced before, and I was treading water, desperately trying to keep afloat.

Chapter 11

A Shitty Time

I was soon to be moved to another room on the ward, and, quite frankly, it was like moving house! Nurses packed up all my cards and other belongings, emptying my bedside cupboard which was full of gifts I hadn't even realised were in there. It's amazing how much you accumulate during a long hospital stay. One of my favourite gifts that still brings a smile to my face was a pair of periscope-like glasses, courtesy of a mystery sender. They were kind of like a lazy person's solution for watching TV if lying flat in bed.

So off I went, clutching my green bag as they wheeled me, and all my belongings, to my new home.

My new surroundings were brighter than the previous room. I was second away from the window on a ward with six beds (including mine), all separated with the familiar sickly cream and lilac-patterned curtains that were faded and worn. Each bed had a simple bedside cabinet and was surrounded by a plinth that housed oxygen outlet pipes and various medical buttons, eradicating any possibility of homeliness. A clock to my right would become my new best friend, checking in numerous times a day whilst waiting for my visits from Martin. The huge windows with reflective film prevented too much sunlight from overheating the room and gave it an unnatural, stifled feel. Oh, how I missed the comfort of my own bedroom right now, with the duck egg blue bedding, matching curtains, and the blissful evening sun when it streamed through the windows catching my feet on the end of the bed. How I missed the view through the window with the golden glow over the surrounding countryside. I would never take it for granted again, I decided.

I was soon to discover Shirley. She was to be my new bedside neighbour to my right. She had the window bed, lucky beggar. Obviously, I was unable to see her, but Martin told me she looked a fair bit older than me. I was surprised to learn that she also had a spinal cord injury.

It was difficult to introduce yourself to people when lying down. Apart from competing with the noise on the ward, I felt invisible, so I didn't bother. Nor did she. I would have plenty of time to get to know Shirley further down the line though.

I was always grateful when I had visitors, and the same question that many asked was

"How do you cope? Don't you get bored?" Well, only a "healthy" person would think such a thing, imagining themselves lying at home in bed after a bout of flu or something. They had no idea! There wasn't time for boredom. When I wasn't fighting to keep pain at bay, I had observations being taken every two hours, and log rolls every three hours. There were visits from spinal nurses and doctors, daily visits from mental health staff, tests, scans, the list went on. I was lucky to find time to sleep.

More recently, nurses would come to take measurements to see how much weight I was losing, which you can tell by how many centimetres you lose from your upper arm. I had lost a considerable amount. Not surprising really; it's true what they say about hospital food. The uninspiring daily meals were worse than school dinners and I couldn't fathom how a hospital could get away with feeding its patients such inedible meals with a lack of anything that vaguely resembled a vegetable. Well... there were those frozen mixed veg portions that are chewy and water-logged, but any nutrients or vitamins had no doubt been zapped out by a microwave. I think the crowning glory for the most unappetizing meal was the fish and chips. A pale-yellow soggy batter on goujon sized pieces of cod (which looked more like a disgusting grey paste) coupled with anaemic-looking chips. I used to take photos to send to Martin, claiming that patients would probably leave sicker than when they had first arrived. For me, however, I think my body knew it needed to get rid of what it already had inside before it could stomach another morsel, so thankfully I had zero appetite. Another conversation with the minions was required, I decided. Heads would roll if they didn't sort themselves out soon!

One day, a dear friend of ours, Dan, came to visit. Now Dan is a bit of a joker, taking the mickey out of me at any given opportunity. It wasn't long before he had me in fits of giggles, much to the annoyance of the duty nurse who was trying to take my blood pressure. She was quite stern as she told me off, insisting it would affect my blood pressure result. This made me and Dan giggle even more. Oh, it felt good to laugh.

We had barely started our catch-up when nurses suddenly appeared from all directions to whisk me off for another unannounced scan. This meant I had to be log-rolled onto a slide board and transferred onto a trolley bed to be wheeled down to radiography. It's not an easy process when you have a fragile back, and every movement made me whimper. I was particularly unhappy that they wouldn't let me take my green bag let alone the fact they had interrupted my visit with Dan. To try and keep my spirits up, he raced alongside me as I was wheeled off to radiography.

Now poor Dan was a little concerned as to why I was having this scan and in the absence of Martin felt he should ask one of the nurses if everything was okay,

'Yes,' came the reply. 'We're just doing a scan for the rings.'

'Rings?'

'Yes, the rings that she swallowed.' Now Dan is a very close friend, almost like family, and Martin had made him aware of the psychosis. But alarmed by this new piece of information, he immediately phoned Martin to tell him that apparently, I had swallowed some rings, and did he know? Oh, how we laugh about this now. The look on his face still makes me snigger.

So, the scan showed the rings were sitting halfway down my duodenum and they didn't appear to be causing a blockage. Clinicians seemed confident that they would continue to pass through my intestines when my bowel movements finally got moving and so it was decided that no intervention was required, for now.

Well, my bowels hung on for three long weeks in total. I was more than desperate to get my first poo over and done with for both physical and mental relief. In the same way a woman grows used to the idea of childbirth after carrying for nine long months, I was now as ready as I could be to do this horrible deed.

The prequel to the main show was pretty mediocre. I passed an amount the size of a Malteser after a manual evacuation which is more unpleasant than most procedures I've experienced as a woman, so that's saying something. Seemingly unsatisfied with my result, the nurse went in for seconds. Now, this is probably as low as things go: when I gave birth to my first daughter some thirty years ago, I had an epidural that numbed me from the waist down to the point of near paralysis. Epidurals were new in those days and they weren't so great at tapering the level to still maintain some sensation. When it came to the second stage of labour I had struggled for many hours trying to push her out when the nurse said to me,

'Just bear down and push Nicola; imagine you're having a poo.' Well, here I was now with four nurses all standing around me saying:

'Come on, Nicola, just give a little push; you're doing really well.'

'Stop!' They all froze, including the nurse whose finger was still up my rear end.

'Get your finger *out* of my bottom now!' The nurse obeyed my command, giving me a gentle stroke on the shoulder before leaving and said we would try again tomorrow. Over my dead body!

The remaining nurses who rolled me back to safety tried to comfort me as I sobbed into the pillow trying hard to keep my distress from the rest of the ward who had probably heard everything that had just happened anyway. I put my headphones on and lost myself in "The Well-

Tempered Clavier" (the "Ave Maria" theme tune). I couldn't even bring myself to share this experience with Martin, it was so degrading.

But then it happened. The day finally arrived, the minions finally fixed the barrier gates and the backlog of three weeks of poo started to make its exit. Like some tectonic landslide, a huge slurry of unstoppable mud would just cascade down the mountainside, continuously. No sooner had I been cleaned up when it started again.

I had sensation "down there" which I kept being told by Martin was a good thing, but it didn't feel like it to me. He received a torrent of texts which, instead of showing the much-awaited relief, displayed the horror of my new humiliating dilemma. It was terrifying: each time I felt it all gushing out, it felt like it was sneaking down the back of my legs towards my knees, and I feared would soon be coming out the end of my bed for all to see. Do bear in mind that lying flat on your back with a thin white sheet over you does exacerbate the sensations and I felt extremely vulnerable. Even so, I must be exaggerating a little since I don't recall the nurses washing my feet!

I was mortally embarrassed, ringing my buzzer and asking the nurse to round up the troops to roll me for a "change". Therein lies one of my problems, communicating to the nurses that I needed a change or "clean-up", as I would call it. I couldn't bring myself to say, "I've pooed myself" or "My nappy needs changing" so I would invariably say 'I need a *clean-up*, please.'

Now some stupid nurses (usually agency) would interpret this "clean" as me wanting to wash my face, returning with a bowl of water and a toothbrush to clean my teeth. Seriously? Others would leave me for quite some time stewing in my poo, not prioritising me because they thought I just wanted a freshen up. I would eventually point out on their second or third return, 'I've had a *poo* and need cleaning up, okay?' For God's sake, surely I shouldn't have had to spell it out so everyone on the ward would know? The experienced, more regular nurses, on the other hand, knew just by the expression on my face what was required.

I would find it so hard not to cry as the nurses (male and female) would roll me over to start cleaning me; they seemed unaware of how difficult it was for me. As if things couldn't get any grimmer, my period started at this time too. I spent hours worrying about how to communicate this, as I didn't want to be cleaned by a male nurse. It really couldn't get any more degrading.

For three long days, this slurry continued every couple of hours, right up until the point I would go to sleep at night and finally get some respite from it. It was exhausting, and I'm sure I lost over a stone in those three days. I suppose if nothing else, this initial onslaught served to get me over my new toilet embarrassment more quickly— the indignity of being changed like a helpless baby seven to eight times a day.

With time, some nurses (the better ones) would talk to me, trying to distract me from what was happening and, sensing my embarrassment during a clean-up, would reassure me that it was no big deal, which it wasn't for them. Others would even make me laugh and, towards the end of my hospital stay, my favourite nurse, Rachel, would play songs to me on her mobile and sing (very badly) to me.

Now my green bag wasn't my only new trigger for near OCD behaviour; before a clean-up I insisted one of the nurses had to spritz some of my Tropic "poo spray" in the air to save the whole ward from any smells and to generally mask my total embarrassment. The glass bottle of toilet spray remained on my trolley table ready for each clean-up.

My tummy returned to its normal size, but my relief at the initial wave of bowel movements and calm that it brought me was short-lived as the bad news followed that my horizontal position meant I would continue to have daily bowel care; with laxatives plus a putrid drink called Laxido that made me gag. How long for, nobody seemed to know, not even my spinal nurse could give me the answers I wanted. I guessed that so long as I was lying flat, my bowels couldn't work effectively on their own due to lack of gravity.

I thanked my Minions for getting things moving but insisted that they now start to slow things down. The runaway train needed to stop! They needed to adjust the level crossings so that the barriers were put back down to give me some rest.

As I lay there with my hands placed over my stomach, I knew the one thing they couldn't help me with was getting the damn rings to make their exit. Each time the nurses had changed my nappy pad, I was aware of their coded language to each other asking if there was any sighting of the rings. They had clearly been asked to keep a close eye out for them. I was mortified! The sooner I could get rid of the damn rings, the sooner I could be free of the last lingering reminder of just how crazy and broken my mind had been.

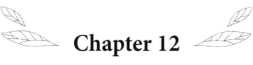

Chapter 12

The Good, the Bad and the Whingey

"It gives me the greatest pleasure to announce that our incredible Nikki Rodwell has achieved her very own ticket to Cambodia & Vietnam! You've worked so hard for this, Nikki, all the groundwork you had put in initially has paid off and your fabulous team came together and helped get you over the finish line, immensely proud."

It was quite surreal seeing this on the screen of my iPhone whilst laying there in the centre of the hustle and bustle of Gately Ward, waiting for my bowel care to arrive. I had done it! I had achieved the next big trip. And with time to spare as well! My boss was congratulating me on Facebook for all to see; there were already dozens of comments and well wishes. I was bursting with excitement and needed to share.

I messaged Martin, who was delighted for me, but up to his eyes in breakfast orders already.

"I'll call you when I can," he messaged back. But knowing that holidaymakers started filling up the café from eight o'clock and that it would likely remain full to the brim until closing time, I knew this was highly unlikely.

Chapter 12

So, I felt somewhat isolated with my fabulous news, and decided I would share it with every nurse that came to my bedside that day. I even shared mid clean-up during my bowel care, almost seeming more acclimatized to this humiliating procedure now.

'So, I've won this trip to Cambodia and Vietnam with my work,' I declared, my face uncomfortably squished towards the bottom corner of my bedside cabinet. Now, this was *not* the way I would ever have expected to be sharing such news! This time last year when I had won the safari trip, I had arrived home to prosecco and flowers from Martin who was ready to celebrate my success with me. Plus, there were an abundance of drinks parties to celebrate with the team as well. But here I was, sharing the news with nurses who were kindly cleaning my backside and finding myself wondering whether I would be "walking-ready" rather than "bikini-ready" by next January. Would they even take me if I was in a wheelchair? Would I be an inconvenience?

As I was log rolled back to my default position, the nurses asked what I did for a job to have won such a fantastic experience. I told them about my Tropic business, and they all laughed… moaning that they were most definitely in the wrong job. Gosh yes, it was quite an eye-opener for me; having never stayed in a hospital before I was quite shocked by the reality of what nurses do, which confirmed what I already knew: it was something I couldn't do in a million years. Yes, these dedicated nurses *were* probably far more deserving of recognition than I was; it takes a special kind of person to do their job.

Now as if winning the trip wasn't good news enough, I picked up my phone to discover a reply waiting in my inbox from Hal Elrod. It felt like Christmas had well and truly arrived, and I couldn't open it quickly enough. My heart sank a little when I realised it was actually from his secretary writing on his behalf to thank me for my email, but I was soon lifted again to see she had attached a video message from him. Damn! I was unable to open it. I immediately hit reply to send a message back asking for it in another format. Oh my god! A video. I tried not to build my hopes up and told myself it was probably a standardised message that was sent out to all of his fans. I hardly dared imagine that he had made a personal video for me, but standard or not, I secretly hoped I would get my email returned that same day with the video in a format that I could watch. It was like being given a beautifully-wrapped present and then being told to wait before being allowed to open it.

It wasn't long before I sobered up from my exciting news. I was just sharing details of the trip with my morning nurse (one whom I nicknamed Flossie due to her blonde fluffy over-bleached hair that looked like candy floss) when she expressed her concern at how tender my calves were, in particular the left one. I winced as she tried to pull my surgical sock up, just as I had been doing all week. I had mentioned more than once to various nurses that my legs hurt since the electronic compression devices had been removed. Flossie wasn't happy to let this continue any longer though and went to discuss it with a more senior nurse. I'm so grateful she did.

I was whisked down for yet another scan. My instinct already knew they would be looking for a blood clot, but I didn't think they would find one. I joked with the radiographer saying how he looked like a young version of Bruce Willis.

'I'll take that.' He laughed. Oh, if I was twenty years younger!

After scanning my thigh, for what only felt like a few seconds, he announced he had found what he was looking for.

'What, in my thigh?' I said, my face dropping and my flirtatious air disappearing

'Actually, I take back what I said, you don't look like Bruce Willis at all…' my efforts to jest could not disguise my upset at learning that I had indeed formed a blood clot in my left leg. It terrified me and took a great deal of consoling from various nurses to reassure me that I wasn't in imminent danger of dropping dead from a stroke. I'm really not very brave when it comes to medical things, a complete wimp in fact!

Sherri, the spinal nurse, made a special visit to see me having heard I was a bit concerned. She took the time to explain things and reassure me that the high dose of anti-coagulant which would be injected into my tummy every night would sort me out. Apparently, the DVT was caused by a combination of the trauma to my body and the lack of mobility. Once feeling a little calmer, I asked Sherri if there was any news on my transfer to Sheffield. She calmly told me I was still sixth on the waiting list and that there was nothing she could do to speed things up. It felt hopeless; I had been here for weeks now and not moved up a single place in the queue. This made me more determined to focus on building the strength in my legs; perhaps going home straight from here was my best option.

Now I really enjoyed physio, it gave me a sense of purpose and some direction in my limited little world. I would feel a sense of smug satisfaction showing the physio girls the results of my hard work, knocking their leg exercises out of the park. I had been practising sliding my leg out and in like scissors, albeit I could only do it with the leg resting on a plastic bag making it easier to slide. I say leg singular because this exercise was too advanced for my left leg at the moment. But progress was happening; my right hip was starting to do its job again.

All of the physiotherapists were amazing and I still think of them all fondly today; there wasn't one that I didn't get on with. The two ladies that came together today were going to be bombarded with my questions concerning the stages of learning to walk again. Nobody had really taken the time to explain this to me, highlighting my simplistic idea of telling the world I would take twenty steps by the end of August. The next stage would be having the back of my bed slowly raised. I was surprised to learn that this, apparently, can be quite tiring, and uncomfortable as the angle is increased. Pah! What could be tiring about sitting? Then, depending on how long that stage took, once I got to around sixty degrees, they would look at the next stage of lifting me to sit up on the edge of the bed. Wow, my back would come off the bed! My feet would touch the floor again. Once that had been practised a few times, I could stand using a frame or they would use a hoist to plant me in the chair beside my bed. It became blatantly obvious that I had a lot of ground to cover in just two weeks.

'That doesn't sound too promising for me to reach my goal then,' I said.

I explained how I wanted to take some steps by the end of August. I didn't think I'd better mention that I'd planned to take twenty… it seemed a little ambitious right now. I shared how much of my motivation came from Hal Elrod, *my hero*, that he had emailed me, and I was waiting for a video from him. I promised them I would work hard and showed them my exercise chart, which they had apparently never seen anything like before. I felt a bit like the class geek!

'So, what do you think?' I asked, hoping for some validation in my quest to take steps in two weeks' time.

I received lots of tactful reassurance and oodles of praise, clearly having surprised them both with my progress. However, they obviously didn't want to burst my bubble. They didn't want to commit to sharing my goal of the end of August probably because they knew I was being overly optimistic. But also, because they were waiting for the go-ahead that I was even allowed to start the next stage.

Now I'm dreadful with names at the best of times, but my brain was even more addled while I was in the hospital. I kept yet another notebook to write down details of things that were said to me and by whom, to relay back to Martin. I had been told by one of the spinal doctors (whose name I clearly forgot to put in the book) just over a week ago, that if my legs were still showing signs of improvement at my next assessment, then they would leave me for a further week on flat bed rest. Huh? My brain could not compute this. It sounded like a punishment for doing well. My only way to get to my goal was for him to give the go-ahead at my three-week checkpoint to start the process of sitting up. Well, here I was three weeks in and waiting. I nagged

Sherri to chase him up for me, secretly convincing myself that I would soon be sitting up like Shirley, my next-door neighbour.

I was a little intrigued by Shirley. I couldn't see her, but could hear conversations from the other side of the drawn curtains, which people (including myself) strangely seemed to think blocked out sound. When her consultant visited, or Sherri was on her rounds, I could hear everything being said if my headphones weren't on, and yes, I may have removed them mid-song to eavesdrop occasionally!

It appeared that she had suffered some kind of bleed on her cervical spinal cord which had caused paralysis from the waist down, like me. However, her left arm was incapacitated, and I found myself feeling suddenly grateful for the use of both my arms. I guess things are relative, but being able to hold my mobile phone or kindle or even just putting my Tropic lip balm on every half an hour seemed like a luxury I couldn't live without right now.

Shirley had been in a little longer than me and it was apparent that she was further ahead in her recovery, already being allowed to have her bed raised to twenty degrees (I found myself feeling strangely jealous of this). I was soon to discover that she complained... a lot. It seemed she would moan about all the things I would think about inside but not say out loud (well, except to Martin perhaps). She would complain if they served her food too slowly, if she was fed up waiting for her bed bath or the light was too bright, and the curtains making her too hot. Yes, she was a whinger and soon began to grate on my nerves. I was trying so hard to be positive and upbeat and soon found my tolerance wearing thin with her constant complaining.

I was being cleaned up after bowel care one morning, four nurses surrounding me, when she moaned through the curtain:

'Are you going to be much longer?' She was waiting for a nurse to finish getting her dressed and change her bedding so thought she should have one of mine instead!

The nurses were already stressed. They would share their work whinges across the top of me as they cleaned me up. Now don't get me wrong, I know each of them had valid reasons for their complaints; stressed with their endless rounds of bed baths and other mounting jobs often meaning they wouldn't get a break. I did feel sorry for them but wished they would save their complaints for the staff room as it made me feel so guilty. I hated to add to their burden, feeling greedy at having four of them to myself. There was no guilt when it came to Shirley though, she could wait her turn!

They looked at each other as she said from the other side of the curtain, 'Why does she always get things first, and please don't pull the curtain between us it makes me too hot.' My internal voice wanted to scream, 'Shirley, believe me, love, if the curtain is opened right now you would think night-time had come with a total eclipse of my arse!'

Another time when my curtain was pulled around for privacy was when the mental health ladies popped down for their daily chat. They took it in turns to visit and so long as they managed to catch me outside of being dressed, washed, having bowel care or physio, they would swap chairs with my lovely assistant to sit and chat with me.

Ruth arrived, another one of my favourites, young enough to be my daughter and always delightful to talk to.

She was always so impressed with my progress and told me that they were planning to pop down every other day from now on since I was doing so well.

I signalled to her to stop talking when I heard Shirley speaking to a nurse. She was complaining about me again and asking why my curtain needed to be pulled. It made me so mad. In fact, it became the instigator to drive me for a better recovery than her. It fuelled the competitive streak in me, which to be honest isn't that hard to ignite. I've inherited much of my competitiveness from my father, who used to challenge me endlessly as a child with backgammon competitions, table-tennis games and even the fun game of who could hold their breath for the longest underwater in our swimming pool. Yes, I would show that whingy bloody woman; I would be up and walking out of here before her.

Sadly, my hopes were soon dashed when the man whose name I forgot arrived for my assessment. It seemed my hard work was paying off and there were definite signs of improved strength in both of my legs. I've never had a good poker face, and this was no exception. When he announced that I was to remain on flat bed rest for another bloody week, making it four in total, I somehow forced a smile as he left, nodding in fake agreement that I understood it was a good thing in the long run, but this conflicted with my inner turmoil. My urgency to start walking or at the very least get into a wheelchair, would not allow for this delay. I was starting to think I may just go crazy (again) if things didn't progress soon. Every inch of my body ached to get home to Martin and my dogs. It was as though I was underwater, holding my breath, and nobody was letting me come up for air.

Poor Martin got another desperate call from me sobbing, but he couldn't talk…

'We'll talk more later, hun, but you can do it. We can get through this.' Hmmm. We? I hated the fact that I was almost starting to resent how his life was continuing. We had two weddings to go to this month which I had been so looking forward to, and now he would be attending without me. It just wasn't fair! And now it felt like salt had been rubbed in the wound being sentenced to another full week of staring at the square panels on the ceiling and counting how many marks I could find; my aching arm having to awkwardly hold my phone up above my face. I felt my chest tighten with the stress. The frustration was too much to bear, especially since I'd overheard physio saying Shirley was sitting at thirty degrees now. I needed to overtake her! My emotions were close to spilling over like that of a spoilt child who had just been told they couldn't go to a party.

Half an hour later, Sherri came sweeping into the ward for her morning checks and came straight to me. As she drew the curtains, almost tearing them off the rail in her usual hurried manner, I tried to hold the tears back as I told her I was to remain on flat rest for another week. She assured me that this was great news and the best thing for me. God, if I heard this one more time I would explode! Why didn't anyone seem to understand? *I* knew what was best for me and that wasn't to be wasting my life away in here. Summer was slipping by and we were eating into August now, with my deadline edging closer each day.

'Any news where I am on the list for Sheffield?' I asked, trying to change the subject.

'You've dropped down to seventh position, I'm afraid.'

What? I'd moved *down* the queue. This news was too

bleak to take in; yet more salt in the wound. On seeing my confusion, Sherri went on to explain that people from all around the country were on the list waiting for their slot just like me. If a person was taken ill or had some other complication, they were temporarily removed from the list. Once recovered, they could then be slotted back in at the same position that they had left. This was what had happened, hence pushing me further down the queue. In three sodding weeks, I had made no headway. I felt the frustration with every inch of my body. I lay there in total disbelief, trying to numb my emotions and focus on my breathing. I was failing miserably.

Martin swept into the ward beaming from ear to ear, so pleased to see me later that afternoon. I soon burst his bubble.

'But I have to stay flat like this another fucking week… I can't bear it. *And* guess what?'

I told him about Sheffield, and he seemed unperturbed. It was all fine, apparently.

'Well, I'm not staying in here till Christmas, which is how it's looking. I'm going to take those steps by the end of August, then I'm out of here. Besides, I've got Glammies to go to on the twenty-fourth of September, and I'm not missing *that.*'

The Glambassadors… Glammies for short: the next big Tropic event at Birmingham NEC. I had to be there to see my girls going up on stage for recognition plus my team had hit their first one million sales threshold so I would get recognition for this, possibly from Lord Sugar himself. No way was I going to miss it!

I received that familiar frown of disapproval from Martin which told me I should be realistic and that he

135

wasn't prepared to discuss it. I spent the rest of his visit with my arms crossed in a childish huff.

'Well, this is great, coming all this way to see you and you're like this.' Despite him having a valid point I couldn't contain my emotions any longer…

'Well, you try lying flat on your fucking back 24/7 with nurses that leave you to stew in your own shit, unable to do anything without asking for help. I'll gladly swap places with you.'

I felt guilty but there was no outlet for my frustration, so yet again, I used Martin as my punch bag. He was getting used to this, learning to take the blows so darn well. However, he was tired and seeing there would be no consoling me, decided to leave.

'Don't bother coming back… I'm doing fine without you!' I lied.

God, the nurses must have thought I was such a bitch.

This final week of lying flat was probably my worst. I'm not a patient person and I was proving to be a very impatient patient. I had no hope in sight for moving to Sheffield where everyone kept telling me I had to go in order to be able to learn to walk again. Shirley was driving me crazy with her whinging and highlighting exactly where I wanted to be right now with sitting up and moving closer to walking again. My patience was tested to its limit and not wanting to *whinge* to the mental health ladies on their daily visits or to the nurses who already had so much to deal with, it was all saved for poor Martin.

It was Sunday morning and I had been staring at the clock in disbelief as the minutes turned into hours. Martin was getting angry messages demanding that I go private (sounds like Margo again, I know); well, I felt like I was being neglected, no one had come to give me my morning wash and change. It was the weekend so it was chaotic, and there were no familiar faces, just agency nurses who seemed to be everywhere except in *our* room. My buzzer was on permanent call, and nobody was coming. My only way to get through the day was by having my little ritual of skincare, body wash and change of gown; it was a necessity, not a luxury. It got to lunchtime and I refused even a single mouthful of food as I was too distressed. My angry messages to Martin were futile as I could hear phones being left to ring out in the nurse's station. Finally, at around 2.00 p.m., a nurse arrived to give me my wash.

'Don't bother now,' I said with my headphones on… trying to block her out from my world, cutting off my nose to spite my face. The agency nurse shrugged and walked away, sensing my upset. How I managed to hold back the frenzy of feather-spitting fury that was inside me I do not know.

I can see looking back that I was probably quite selfish, unaware that others may have had needs more important than mine. It was something Martin would remind me of, but at the time it meant nothing to me. I had no concept of others' difficulties, I was just trying to survive my own, as best as I could, and the weekends would test me to my limit!

However, I was soon to learn that there was another way; in the midst of my life's biggest challenge, I would find an inner strength that I didn't know I had.

I was ecstatic to hear back from Hal Elrod, this time with a video that worked. Now not many can comprehend this, but it was more exciting for me than receiving the news of winning the trip to Cambodia. I had finally received a video from the man himself; not a standard video sent to all his fans either! There he was on my mobile phone clear as daylight talking to me personally!

'Hi, Nikki' he said, in his strong American accent. He acknowledged that my injury "did not sound like fun and must be a *pretty tricky* situation to be in", well yes, that was one way of putting it. But then he said what an amazing opportunity it could turn out to be for growth and development. He said that these challenges bring us a great opportunity. It was a "gift". Wow. Not something I'd planned to put on my Christmas list!

He touched on his own adversities and said that *his* success had been due to his level of acceptance. He realised that when he was in the hospital with eleven broken bones and some brain injuries too, that if he could *accept* and learn to be his happiest right at that moment when things couldn't be any worse, then he could *always* find happiness and be the best version of himself in any given situation. Literally, during his hospital stay, after numerous surgeries and being told it would take one year to recover, he was laughing and joking with the nurses, leading everyone to believe he was delusional and not accepting the nature of his injuries when he was. He realised that to have the most successful recovery possible he needed to accept his "now" and be his best.

I re-watched him again and again, smiling. Oh my god, he was talking to me and telling me that I could turn my situation into a success story too. I couldn't stop watching it. The video was just a few minutes long, but the message started to become clear. I had a light bulb moment. This predicament had been sent to me for a reason. There were lessons in this for me too. There was nobody and nothing to blame, I realised. It didn't matter how or even why it had happened; these thoughts were only holding me back, as were the feelings of frustration and anger each time I had a setback or a bad day. No, it was possible to embrace this like nothing else in my life. I could let go of *all* my anger and frustrations and start to journey through my bear hunt being the best version of myself whatever the outcome. But first off, I realised this would mean I needed to stop firing off all my complaints at Martin. I needed to find a better level of tolerance and not give credence to all my frustrations by ranting at him. I could see that whilst I was very efficient with my goal setting and physical determination, these were only part of my journey. I needed to change my attitude and find a better, kinder way of being.

I lay there and tried to find a way to say goodnight to Martin with an apology, and wrote a poem which is totally not my style…

As I lay down to sleep,
I focus on breathing in so deep.
As I release tension and fear as well,
I untie the knots which make me yell.
My last thought before I drift off to dream,
Is of my life's greatest love, which is you it would seem.
To dream of the time we will have to come,
In Coco Bay and drinking rum.
Love you. Sorry. XX

Chapter 13

Fellowship of the Rings

The middle of the hottest August ever and a hospital ward with no air conditioning was not the best place to be. I counted my blessings though as I imagined poor Martin sweating from head to toe in a painfully small and airless kitchen, frying food all day. At least I had a fan next to me providing comfort with its cool breeze and reassuring hum.

I strained my eyes to look down and see some of the other patients in the room. There were five in total and they had a constant stream of visitors who I caught glimpses of in their pretty summer dresses, sun-kissed faces radiating that buzz of excitement you get when refreshed after holidaying somewhere abroad. I felt envious. Summer was slipping by and leaving me behind. But this didn't deter me from waking up and embracing each day with the determination to not only push myself physically but to find small things to be thankful for (well, apart from the hospital food). I slowly started becoming kinder not only to myself but to the nurses. I took the time to talk to them and get to know them. I even spoke to Shirley, albeit I couldn't see her yet. I shouted across to say hi and commented how we were the oldest kids on the block! During our brief conversation she whinged that she felt we would never get to Sheffield, and I found myself reassuring her. It was apparent that, like me, she wasn't prepared to wait to get there, so was looking at the option of going to a private rehab centre in Cambridge. Now I couldn't afford this option, but Martin assured me this was for the best as it would hinder me from getting to Sheffield.

I tried to stay focused on Hal, whom I felt intrinsically connected to now. Well, I was almost replicating his hospital experience, although it was looking doubtful that I would walk out of here in six weeks. I was over four weeks in now and waiting for the big moment where I was finally to have the back of my bed raised.

That day finally came... My mate Dan was there to share the momentous event with me and took photos for me to splatter all over Facebook. As the nurses slowly raised the back up to ten degrees, they asked me if I was giddy. I wasn't. It was fine, albeit very strange. Your body gets so used to its periphery from lying flat day after day, that it's hard to explain just *how* weird it was to see my world from a completely new angle. I was suddenly able to see things on the ward I hadn't known were there. A sink, a chair, the notes pinned on the ends of the beds in front of me. It felt like I was being lifted back into the land of the living. I was able to smile at people now and they would see me! I was no longer hidden away. I was part of the world again.

'Any signs of the rings, Nick?' Dan laughed.

'No, not yet.' I felt embarrassed but tried to make light of it. I still couldn't quite believe I had swallowed the damn things and was pretty worried they were never going to come out. I had the threat of a gastroscopy hanging over me now, which broke me out in a sweat since I'd been told by so many people that the tube being forced down your throat was extremely painful and unpleasant. The thought filled me with utter dread.

Due to my low blood pressure and the body learning to readjust, I was only allowed to sit up in my new position for about ten minutes. I was given permission to use the bed remote control and instructed to do little and often at first, keeping to a limit of ten degrees.

I was beaming when Martin came bouncing onto the ward a little later, two hours before visiting time. The nurses were flexible with his visits because of the distance he had to come and his commitment with the café. Showing off my new semi-upright position to him, he too was excited as he presented a pink picnic bag to me. It was laden with M&S macaroons, almond croissants, fresh fruit, sausage rolls, in fact an entire picnic hamper. We brought the idyllic seaside picnic to Gately Ward and it was beautiful, even though my appetite still evaded me.

Martin was in one of his enthusiastic need to fix, move and entertain me moods, which was a cross between an over-excited puppy and a party entertainer! Bless him. I was shattered after he went, not because of twenty minutes of sitting up at ten degrees, but the intensity of his visit.

The next day when physio came, I was excited that they felt I was ready to be raised up to twenty degrees as my blood pressure had coped so far. I was progressing in leaps and bounds now. As they raised the back of the bed a little more, I felt my hamstrings tighten up into a stretch that honestly felt like some advanced yoga pose. It hurt, far more than I'd expected. What the hell was going on with my legs? I had to take deep breaths to manage the discomfort, but it wasn't long before I went back down to the safety and comfort of lying flat. Physio spent some time doing my leg exercises with me instead.

Physio left and I felt disappointed. I realised that if I were to have any chance of reaching my goal, which was just ten days away now, I had to tackle this head on. I got to work with my notebook and added three sessions per day of sitting up at twenty degrees for the next few days. I set the goal of ten minutes increasing to fifteen, taunting myself with the need to see neat little ticks of achievement in my notebook. Music was my saviour yet again. I would find a calming piece of music to listen to through my pink headphones and sit there with my hamstrings feeling like they were about to rip. Focused on my breathing with my eyes shut, I willed myself to remain there until the time was up. I would keep opening one eye and peer at the clock. It felt like a lifetime, like an endurance test.

My phone also became a useful distraction from the pain of sitting up. I would save checking my social media and messages until this time, now focusing on reading and responding to posts as well as breathing myself away from the discomfort. It was whilst I was sitting up at twenty-five degrees a few days later when I noticed I had a long-awaited WhatsApp message from Stephanie, my middle daughter, telling me she was sorry for not being in touch or supporting me through this difficult time but that she was having great difficulty in processing what had happened. I found myself wondering whether she was angry with me, perhaps thinking I had tried to end my life. It was difficult to know whether to try to speak to her or not, for fear of there being any upset. I opted for a reply saying that it was fine, and I hoped to speak to her soon. The coward's way to respond, perhaps.

I felt terrible guilt that my children had a mum who had broken again; was I an embarrassment to them? Did my psychosis make me less of a mum than I should be? I knew it wasn't the right time to address this; there was a limit to how much I could face in one go. Relationships had a lifetime to be worked on, I decided, there was no immediate urgency, whereas my recovery... well, the timer was ticking away.

I had been reading up on spinal cord injuries, doing a little homework so to speak, and I had learnt that there are two types of SCI. The levels of injury were referred to as "complete" or "incomplete" and it seemed that with the former, people were paralysed from the point of injury and below, permanently. Incomplete injuries like mine, on the other hand, could be paralysed initially but then get back varying levels of sensation with some being able to walk again. Yes, this was what I thought, this was me! I skimmed over the paragraph that mentioned how some "incompletes" could remain paralysed. Frustratingly, there was no ability to predict someone's level of recovery or likelihood of walking again. Each and every individual was very unique with no two cases ever being recorded the same; we were like snowflakes! All of the recovery seemed to take place in the first two years after injury. I read that the most happened in the first six months, slowing down after a year with no further improvements after the two-year point. This served to make my personal recovery feel even more urgent. Time was ticking away like the countdown to midnight on New Year's Eve and Jules Holland's Hootenanny had already started!

Having side-stepped my conversation with Stephanie, I realised I did need to address the situation with Chloe. She hadn't visited for a while and hadn't been in contact. It was a more pressing matter since she was jetting off to Morocco soon. She was going for a whole year as part of her language degree and was leaving on 1st September. I felt guilty that I had spent the whole summer in here when I could have been having quality mother/daughter time with her which made me feel incredibly sad. I was going to message her and be direct. Things needed sorting, and the elephant in the room needed to be addressed.

Chloe it makes me sad that you don't respond to my messages or comment or even "like" my posts on my progress on Instagram or Facebook. You don't come and visit, which for whatever reason that's okay... but I'm trying so hard to push through the difficulties I am encountering in here, amidst which I try to send you a little bit of love or things to say I'm thinking of you, to which you don't respond. Have I lost you? You don't seem able to find a little space to send me any well wishes or love. (sad face x 2) I miss you. X

The little tick confirmed that it had been sent.

Shirley was now at the stage of sitting up on the edge of her bed. I strained to listen through the curtain whilst physio were guiding her through the process. An invasion of privacy I know, but I was intrigued to know what I had coming to me next. The first time she tried, it had made her feel sick, and they lay her back down almost immediately;

she sounded a little shaken. But a few days later she was sitting with her feet touching the ground! Wow, she was getting so much closer to walking than me. I still had to get to sixty degrees and wasn't even halfway there yet. I was genuinely really pleased for her, but found myself sneaking the bed remote up a few degrees more than I was allowed.

Now whilst I was becoming much calmer and better at coping with difficulties (there was far less complaining to Martin), the one thing I really struggled with and will remember forever was my bowel issues. They really started to play me up and I couldn't help but notice that Shirley didn't seem to have the same problem. The purpose of bowel care was to get the deed over and done with first thing in the morning with just the one clean-up. However, I seemed to drag mine through the entire day with endless clean-ups. It was as if my bowels were a little too over-excited. As were the nurses, in anticipation of "who" would be the one to be cleaning me and have the first sighting of the rings. I think they were placing bets. Embarrassing!

'Nope, not this time.'

'Sshh!' I would glare at them, mortified that someone outside my curtains might hear, like Shirley for example, and wonder what on earth was going on.

Well, the momentous day came, and the rings finally made their exit. The nurse changing me that day thought she'd hit the jackpot and announced their arrival a little too loudly for my liking! I couldn't look the other three nurses in the eye, I was too embarrassed. They asked if I wanted them cleaned up so they could give them back to me. Er, no! I never wanted to see them again, I certainly didn't want to look at them on my fingers knowing where they had been; they would be a reminder of just how crazy I had been. No, I told them to put them straight in the bin.

One of the nurses who remained to put my bed down and strap my green bag back on the side enquired about the rings. So, before you ask the same question the answer is no, they weren't expensive, one was £30 from a market stall and the other was a £15 silver ring. Thankfully I hadn't swallowed anything important like my wedding ring or my white gold diamond wrap ring. I didn't tell the young nurse this though.

'Oh, it was just a ring my grandmother left me in her will, I never really liked it,' I joked.

'Oh my god, did it have diamonds in?' she asked. I was teasing her a little too much and for fear that she may have just gone rummaging through the nappy bin to find them, I told her the truth and we both laughed.

The final goodbye to my rings was a huge relief, not just because I could now avoid the gastroscopy, but, psychologically, I could say goodbye to my psychosis. The last embarrassing reminder had now gone. Sadly though, it didn't do much to relieve me of my bowel difficulties. They became worse on a daily basis and were the most horrendous part of my journey at the Norfolk and Norwich Hospital (N&N), so bear with me a little longer as the minions do retire soon, I promise.

Some days they would drive me to complete despair. I think I had some kind of irritation or perhaps it was my bowel trying to regain its independence, but there was a constant feeling of something trying to come out. However, nine times out of ten, after the nurses gathered to clean me up, there was nothing there or just a rabbit dropping. I felt so bad calling them nonstop to come and check me, but I had no control over what was happening and was more than paranoid about being left with any excrement in my bed. I have no idea what my minions were thinking but they were certainly getting over-enthusiastic and a bit erratic.

It would make me burst into tears on occasions, such as when I felt the urge just as a visitor turned up. Approaching my bed with their "so pleased to see you" face, they were greeted with a look of stricken horror, and I would beg them to go away. Instantly! It must have been confusing for them, and I hope they never thought I didn't appreciate the kindness of their visit, but the distress of my unpredictable bowel movements meant that some days I just could not bear having visitors.

Nobody seemed concerned with my shitty problem, apart from me; Sherri just reduced my bowel care from daily to every other day, which didn't seem to make much difference. I started slipping my laxatives into disused tissues or hiding them in my leftover food since I felt perhaps they were over-stimulating my bowel. Nothing seemed to help, and I just had to fight my way through this struggle almost daily for the remainder of my time at the N&N.

One of the nurses remained behind after yet another clean-up. She had been instructed to change my catheter bag and, as I watched her take off the large plastic bag full of my dark yellow pee, I thought how strange it was. A tube coming out of my lady garden, winding its way down the bed under the sheet, out of the side of the bed at the bottom, and around to the bag hanging via a clip on the front end of my bed. I could see the urine as it moved along the tube and it made me think of the marble run my girls used to play with. Martin and I had nicknamed it Cathy, short for Cathy the Catheter and, luckily for me, he was totally unfazed by all the medical messiness that was involved with my injury, including burst catheters and my bowel predicament.

As the nurse left, I found myself wondering if it bothered other people to see Cathy who was sometimes hooked on the side of my bed when they came to visit. In fact, did it bother Chloe? Was this perhaps one of the reasons she hadn't come back to visit me? It was preying on my mind more and more and I started to convince myself that she probably hated seeing me in hospital. Having to share her visits with Cathy probably grossed her out. I knew she disliked my social media activity too; Martin had hinted she had said as much during a shift in the café. But I wondered if there was something more. What was I missing?

Chapter 14
The Fall

Being woken in the middle of the night with four nurses looking down on me, suited up with aprons and gloves, used to trigger my fight or flight mechanism. As my eyes tried to take in my surroundings and my brain compute where the hell I was, my heart would be pounding in my chest with me having a near panic attack. Well, it was a sure sign that I had started adapting, almost moulding to my new life as I would barely wake up now... letting them roll me like a rag doll to do the checks, then the bed jolting back down to its original position when they finished. I would peer through a half-opened eye to check my green bag had been put back in situ as they left!

My day was ruled by the clock on the wall, starting around five or six a.m. when I would wake, sometimes in need of pain meds, and get stuck into my workout and visualisation routine. I was starting to wean myself off the pain meds as much as possible, missing doses of morphine, cutting out codeine completely and just continuing with the four-hourly paracetamol. I was worried about becoming addicted like the people I had read stories about in magazines and seen in storylines in soaps. Plus, I wanted to stop masking any pain and find out what I was dealing with, which as it turned out, was fairly manageable most of the time. There was a strange nagging sensation in my lower back which seemed nowhere near the site of the injury, but it was easily resolved with a half dose of morphine at night. No, my biggest source of discomfort was the ongoing bowel saga which I dearly hoped reducing my meds may help to resolve.

Now, the comings and goings of new patients on the ward were like a short stay car park. They were brought in, invariably asleep having come straight out of an operation, with their mouths wide open catching flies; two days later the bed was empty awaiting the arrival of its next patient. Some were moved off the ward as soon as the anaesthetic wore off, and sent to a "holding" ward to wait for their discharge. Others stayed a day or two until taken home by relatives once their final blood tests were done. Some days, I would fall asleep for a rest having seen one patient's face, to wake up to that of another in the bed opposite me. It always surprised me how quickly they were pushed out the door with crutches or a walking frame for their broken limbs. There was only one constant on the ward, well, two actually… Shirley and I were firmly parked in the long-stay beds.

The ward was always bustling with visitors and, with my newly-acquired kindness skills, I would smile and chat to other people's visitors should they look my way, sometimes asking them to pass me something I couldn't reach or had dropped. I even found myself smiling at the humanism representative who visited the ward once a week and whom

I had always made sure I had avoided with my head stuck in a book or under my sheet. Of course my smile was taken as an invitation for him to come and talk to me about my beliefs and for him to proudly explain exactly what "humanism" is. It was going pretty well until I showed him a photo of Chloe and he expressed a slightly pervy interest in her.

'Wow, she's stunning, what a looker.' Yes, clearly she was, and this was a normal observation, but when I tried to return to some of my spiritual beliefs to contest his humanism theory of there being no afterlife, he said, 'How about we talk about that gorgeous daughter of yours, when is she coming to visit you?' He was at least my age, possibly even late fifties, so to see the leery look on his face talking about my twenty-one-year-old daughter felt wrong on all levels. Plus, he looked a bit like Chloe's dad, and the less said about that the better. Needless to say, I never encouraged him to engage in conversation with me again.

My dear little Chloe, I was still feeling a little anxious about what was wrong. She knew I had suffered a psychotic episode before so why was she upset? Was she worried that I was going to be disabled perhaps? I broached the topic with Martin when he arrived later that afternoon.

'It's difficult for her,' he said. 'You know how they are with social media at her age.' Yes, I did, there was so much pressure to look perfect, with just the right filter to look flawless in a devastatingly cool pose to keep up with the competition. So, it was the social media that was bothering her. God forgive the embarrassing parent who would post a photo looking half-dead in a hospital gown, with two Pringles sticking out their mouth looking like Donald

Duck for some light entertainment from a hospital bed! Oh, how I love that photo.

'Would she prefer me to tell the world what actually happened then?' I asked.

I wondered if she resented the attention I was receiving on my social media posts because people didn't know the truth. That perhaps I was getting sympathy and support for breaking my back under false pretences and in some way deceiving them. Did she feel it was my fault in some way? Or worse still, did she presume like I feared others may, that I had attempted to take my own life?

'She knows I didn't jump to try to commit suicide, right?'

'Well, she saw you come off the roof with her own eyes,' he replied.

Shit! What? She had seen it? I had thought that Martin was the only one who had been there. I tried to remember, but my brain could only recall snippets; I remembered seeing Martin on the phone in our garden, but Chloe wasn't there, I was sure of it.

'She was out on the road waiting to direct the ambulance in but could see you up on the roof from the road.'

'You're kidding,' I cried, praying that he was.

'The whole bloody village could see you up there from their windows...' It was almost as if he said this for dramatic effect. It worked. The horror that filled me was awful. Tears started streaming down my face. I couldn't believe that my poor daughter had been witness to something so awful. I envisaged her and then the whole village twitching their curtains watching from their windows. It was too much.

'What the fuck?' I cried, becoming increasingly distressed with Martin seemingly oblivious to how this new piece of information had shocked me to the core.

I asked him to leave, but he seemed confused about what he had done wrong.

'Nikki, I think you're over-reacting a little,' he said, refusing to go. I lay there a weepy mess, picturing what poor Chloe must have felt waiting for the ambulance, imagining what she saw. It was then that the veil started to lift. I could hear a distant yapping dog…

As I crouched on top of the outbuilding, I removed my rucksack. There was a tiny black puppy in the garden beneath, yapping away at me hysterically. It seemed like one of those little toy dogs that could do backward flips, but why was it yapping so much? I wished someone would make it shut up and take its batteries out. The occupants must have been out, I thought.

So here I was, sitting on a roof, clutching my rucksack and wondering what I was supposed to do next. It was a bright sunny day with a powder blue sky filled with puffy white clouds which I somehow expected to spread into some formation to send me a message. I looked up, trying to tune my thoughts in to some sort of signal from Radio Gaga, but they were all jumbled up and making no sense; I had no idea how to tackle the obstacle in front of me. How could I get down off this roof and escape? How could I continue with my mission if I didn't get down and through the neighbour's garden?

I was peering over the edge with my foot leaning on the guttering to see how far the shingle was below, when there he was. Martin was standing in our garden calling up to me and my confusion intensified. Whilst he looked like

Martin, it wasn't my husband. I didn't even want a husband right now. He had a phone in his hand and was speaking to someone. I then remembered he was my enemy, confirmed by the fact he called up to me that an ambulance was on its way and to hold on. He continued talking to someone on the phone, unaware that I was looking at him. I tried desperately to make the connections in my brain work, to find the right thing to say to him. There was a split second where I wanted to call to him for help, a fleeting second of sanity when I wanted to cry out to tell him that I was trapped and didn't know what to do… but he was telling them about me. Whoever he was speaking to, he wanted them to come and take me away, to put me in "that" place. Oh God, time was running out, what was I to do?

I turned myself towards the pitch of the roof, as I heard a voice saying to me that I had got it all wrong. I didn't have a special mission or message to deliver. It was a sinister message that I was bad, evil, *I* was the enemy and everyone else was good. I had been dropped to earth by accident. Horror filled me as I realised that I was a mistake; God's fallen angel. I was a bad person. As thoughts jumped around trying to make connections, I started to believe that my dad was God, why else did he have the name 'father' too? I began clambering on my hands and knees towards the pitch of the roof, feeling like a trapped animal. I froze as I reached the ridge, a flashback of childhood washed over me, a time when I was around ten years old…

My dad used to hold me by the wrists and dangle me from the diving board over our swimming pool when I was a girl. I would lean back in such a way that if he were to let go, I would fall. We called it the trust game. It was dangerous and exciting. I would always say 'Please don't let me fall, Dad,' entrusting him with my safety. He would dare me to do this in various locations such as over the edge of a low cliff or leaning out from a ridge of some kind. But on this particular occasion, my parents had close friends over and it became our party piece. Dad and I decided to show off our risky game from the diving board whilst I was fully clothed, adding the danger of me getting wet if I fell in.

'You *will* catch me?' I asked, as always.

'Do you trust me?' he would say, and let go of one wrist, grabbing the other moments before I fell back far enough to fall into the pool. He continued with this for about thirty seconds, swapping from one arm to the other, just like he had done all the other times. But then, on this occasion with the friends watching, he had dropped me in, fully clothed. I was instantly shocked by the cold, dark, wetness of the pool, gasping for breath as I surfaced. This had never happened before.

I threw a massive tantrum and screamed at him as I heaved myself out of the pool in my sodden jeans and t-shirt, feeling humiliated as everyone laughed, presuming this was part of the act. He had let me go!

After I had got changed, my dad had got angry with me for my little outburst, telling me that I had failed to grab his wrist, that it was *my* fault. He said that I had deliberately let myself fall in the pool.

Well, here I was at fifty-two years old, picturing the whole episode as if it happened yesterday, clutching on to the roof. My crazy mind saw the whole event flash before me with a voice questioning me as to who had let go of who but then in fact telling me that it was *me* who had not grabbed his wrist. I was wicked for having blamed him and causing such a scene since the fault lay with me. But hang on a minute, rack your brain, Nikki, how had it really happened?

Martin was calling up to me again, but I couldn't look at him. I had to focus. If I got this right everything would make sense, I was sure of it. My dad always told me to relax and let *him* grab my wrists first. 'Don't flinch,' he would say. My thoughts spun. Was it him or was it me? I leant backwards with my arms out in front of me, believing that someone or something would catch me this time to give me the answer to my question. As I leant back, I plunged into oblivion.

I plummeted backwards, hitting the partitioning flint wall between our neighbours' gardens before I landed face up on the shingle beneath, my arms and legs sprawled out in an "s" shape.

The yapping of the puppy stopped. Everything went quiet.

I sobbed as the memory came flooding back to me, now realising the full extent of what had happened. I had been in a state of utter confusion, feeling trapped, and the psychosis had been playing tricks with me. I could not find the words to explain all this to Martin. It was too much. I was overwhelmed with shock and sadness but there was also a tinge of relief. The final piece of the jigsaw was in place and I now understood that I had fallen back from the roof, not jumped.

Martin didn't understand why he had upset me so much. He admitted that he may have exaggerated a little when saying the entire village had witnessed the event; that probably just the neighbours whose garden I had borrowed, and our other immediate neighbour had seen it, but it made no difference. I was finding it hard to process; both the new detail *and* the way in which he had told me. Knowing how my precious daughter had witnessed this, and feeling totally wretched, I pushed him away; craving to be alone to find my own way to try to come to terms with it.

After he left, I pressed my button to call a nurse, who looked shocked to see I had been crying. I asked her to put in a request for someone from Mental Health to come and see me that evening, and I really hoped it would be Gemma. I had been told that I could call them anytime, but this was the first time I felt the need. I needed to talk this through.

As it would turn out, I was in luck and it was Gemma who came to sit with me for a chat a little later on. I stuttered through my sobs, opening up to her about the fall from the roof. I even surprised myself as the words fell so easily from my mouth.

'I just let myself fall backwards, but I didn't know what I was doing...'

I told her how I had such an amazing life, that there was no way on earth I had planned to take my own life. I went on to explain about the BWRT and how it had made my eyes flicker and my brain shudder. Gemma was making notes as the words continued to gush from my mouth. She seemed particularly interested in the BWRT treatment, scribbling away, trying not to miss any details.

'But why would he be such a bastard and tell me everyone was watching?' I sobbed, trying to pull the focus away from the BWRT which didn't matter anymore. Gemma was brilliant at comforting me and telling me how brave I had been. She said that I was astounding everyone with my recovery, especially the mental health team. She agreed that Martin had been tactless but also that he probably found it difficult to realise just how traumatic it was for me to have remembered it all. As she reassured me, I felt the tightness loosen in my chest and the little tic I get in my throat when stressed started to subside.

I continued opening up my heart to Gemma, telling her about the difficulties I have in my relationships with my daughters and how I feared that Chloe now seemed to be pulling away from me and that I couldn't cope with this prospect right now; not whilst I was still feeling vulnerable and weak. She questioned my concerns about social media and encouraged me to continue posting if the support from my friends helped me, telling me not worry if it bothered Chloe since she could always remove me from her social media.

After I had calmed down, Gemma and I agreed that if I still felt any remnants of anxiety or sadness in an hour's time, I should have a tranquiliser, something to help relax me and enable a good night's sleep (as much as possible with three-hourly log rolls). Gemma wrote on my medical notes to allow me diazepam if I requested and then we said goodbye, with me thanking her for everything and assuring her I would be fine now.

As it turned out, I was, and the diazepam was not required. I was silently proud of how quickly I pulled myself out of this burst of anxiety. By listening to my "calm" app and focusing on my breathing, I let go of the embarrassment of the village seeing my crazy actions and the worry that I might be losing Chloe. After all, we could always move if the neighbours *had* seen it, I told myself, and Chloe would come round. I would talk to her.

Alina, a lovely dark-haired nurse, came to do my final blood pressure and observations before I went to sleep. As she put the familiar black sleeve on my arm, I noticed she wore a white uniform with blue piping, which signalled she was an agency nurse. I was surprised therefore that she was quite chatty and showed an interest in me. As she checked my blood pressure, I told her how I yearned to get my hair washed and she hinted that she would investigate to see what she could do about this.

After final meds at 9.45 p.m. and the routine little injection in my tummy, I settled down with my headphones on to block out the noise of buzzers, nurses' chatter and the moans and groans of patients on the ward. I found my classical playlist which I found to be the most relaxing genre to drift off to sleep to. Yes, classical was the best for soothing difficult emotions too. Music can be so therapeutic, and I started to discover a magical quality about it that I hadn't noticed before. Take "Moonlight Sonata", for example, that famous classic which I have heard so many times in my life, and even played it on the piano. It took on a new dimension now. I had never truly listened to the beautiful key change and climax before the ending, which literally brought tears to my eyes and transported me to a blissful state. I made myself a promise: that when I was finally home, I would learn this piece to the end. I was renowned during my piano playing days for never learning pieces to the end and this piece was no exception. I quickly put this out to my accountability partner in a goodnight post on Facebook and then the final remnants of my stress and anxieties melted away with the sombre tones of "Moonlight Sonata" as I drifted off to sleep.

Chapter 15

Rock Bottom Has a Basement

After a restless night, I was surprised to be woken at 5.30 a.m. by Alina telling me to 'ssh' with her finger over her mouth, so as not to wake the sleeping patients on the ward. In her broken English, she told me she was going to wash my hair for me. Now I don't know why she was so kind, putting herself out for me in this way. Perhaps she didn't like the sight of my greasy locks? I don't know, but I am indebted to her. Like a couple of naughty schoolchildren in a boarding school dormitory, we quietly set about the long-overdue task of washing my hair. This involved a plastic blow-up sink, like a mini paddling pool, which she wedged under my head, whilst I held a towel around me to prevent getting water everywhere. Jugs of blissfully warm water anointed my scalp and trickled down my neck as she massaged my head and washed away the weeks of dirt and grime from my hair. I closed my eyes and immersed myself in every second of this indulgence as dawn broke through the curtains.

As I lay there with my damp hair, feeling strangely normal and almost like I was a step closer to home now,

I checked my phone. I had a message from Chloe! She said that she wanted to maintain a relationship with me and that I wouldn't lose her (that was a relief). She said things weren't fine, that there was a great deal of hurt and anger, but she hadn't said anything for fear of causing me further distress. She said she was appearing aloof due to conflicting emotions she was finding it difficult to deal with and yes, Facebook and social media were embarrassing and unnecessary in her opinion.

I felt such a mixture of feelings. Text messages are so hard to interpret. Well, I read this message over and over again, trying to read between the lines, but I just needed to know that she and I were still friends, that she loved me even a fraction of how much I loved her. She was obviously struggling, and I felt awful for that, but I didn't know what I had done to make her angry with me, and since she wasn't going to give me clarity, I just felt confused. I didn't want complicated right now, I just wanted good old-fashioned love and kindness. I would ask Mr Fix-it when he came to visit that evening.

Martin was sitting with me sharing a packet of Pringles at thirty-five degrees (not temperature but bed angle). We were laughing at something when I started to get a real attack of the giggles. We both started laughing uncontrollably until I froze in a panic and glared at him…

'Oh my god, I'm weeing myself.' Our frivolity jolted to a halt. 'Call the nurse or something… this shouldn't be happening.' Now you would have thought I had just said I could feel the baby's head crowning with the way he legged it out the room to go and find the help of a nurse. What had happened apparently, was something called a by-pass.

My urine had taken a detour and by-passed the catheter completely, which, in itself, didn't bother me too much. I was more horrified at the sensation I had felt whilst it had happened, an intense clamping feeling which would turn out to be the oh-so-delightful bladder spasm. Again, it would turn out I was pretty unique here; no one else with catheters seemed to have the same issue.

My bed and I were cleaned up, and knowing Martin was waiting on the other side of the curtain I called out,

'Well, that certainly gives a whole new meaning to PMSL.' I could hear him chuckle. With Cathy back in place and my bed cleaned up, Martin and I had a more serious conversation. He told me how he had come home to find Chloe crying hysterically one evening.

'She was in a real state, Nikki, I had to literally sit and hug her until she stopped shaking.'

I welled up. How had I not seen this from her perspective? How confusing and upsetting it must be for her. Apparently, she was angry because of my having had a psychotic episode before.

'She needs reassurance that it won't happen again, Nikki, we all do.'

Now whilst I had full sympathy at the distress this caused to my nearest and dearest, it also seemed a bit of an unreasonable request to me. It's not like I had any control over the psychosis when it happened. It snuck in like a thief in the night and held me to ransom. How could I anticipate or know if it was to happen again? Thinking back to the other occasions, they too seemed to have come out of nowhere, so I failed to see how I could give a guarantee that it would never happen again. God knows, I *never* wanted it to happen and would do anything to not have to go through it again.

'Just be patient and loving with her, Nikki, it's all you can do, she'll work it out with time'.

Chloe obviously felt a weight had been lifted off her shoulders after sending me her message, and Martin having soothed her distress at home. She sent me a text before her final visit to say that she didn't want to discuss anything heavy and wanted to just spend some pleasant time with me. I had a stomach full of nerves, trying my hardest to keep it together as I couldn't bear the thought that this would be the last time I would see her this year. I think most parents can sympathise with how terrifying it felt to think of my beautiful little princess going off to live in Morocco, albeit with a few other friends from uni.

She came in looking perfect, a petite little bundle of loveliness. My angel. The text messages were firmly swept under the carpet and I sensed it was best to let sleeping dogs lie. We sat and chatted as if nothing had happened, whilst doing a crossword puzzle together before the dreaded moment came when she indicated it was time to leave. The lump in my throat felt like it would choke me, as I told her to be safe, have fun (but not too much) and send me lots of pictures. She hugged me and I could tell she was struggling too. As she left the room she didn't look back, which I was glad of since the tears were streaming down my face.

Five minutes later, the welcome face of Nurse Rachel came bounding onto the ward to hug me and I blubbed in her arms. I smiled through my tears when she told me how Chloe had broken down crying in the corridor too and Rachel had hugged her, promising her that she would look after me. My daughter did care. God, I would miss her so much.

My journey in the N&N was a rollercoaster ride when I look back on it, both physically and emotionally, with the view forever changing. My new distraction during the day was something called bladder training, which may as well be called toilet training since I was similar to a toddler in so many ways. A little junction tap was attached to the tube near the top of my leg with a switch to flick open to let the pee drain away. It was to be clamped for one hour at a time and then released for "free flow" for ten minutes. This was supposed to strengthen my bladder muscle and teach it to hold urine again. It became complicated though since instead of one hour, after a few days I was to increase to two hours. I had to set the alarm on my phone to remind me and also run a timer to remind me when the ten-minute free flow was up! This process was repeated right up until bedtime… or rather *sleep time* since every hour of every day was bedtime for me.

The first problem I encountered with bladder training was breaking the damn tap when I flicked it, or it would come away in my hand, soaking me and my bed in urine. This meant rounding up the Keystone Cops for another change. But then, aside from the difficulties I had with the little junction tap, things started to gradually get worse for my poor bladder, almost as if the lady minions were jealous of all the attention their husbands had been getting with my bowels. They wanted some of the limelight now and were to become another huge obstacle for me to overcome.

My physio was progressing well, and some days I did extra leg exercises straight after our session. My tiny little sparrow legs were not giving me confidence that they were going to be up for the job coming their way. My usual, chunky thighs had vanished, and I almost felt I was on my way to a thigh gap! I was mid-leg-raise when my bloody catheter split again and came apart, letting pee flood all over my bed. I pressed my buzzer for a nurse, and at the very same moment in swept Katy, a friend from our drama society. I stopped her from kissing me.

'Please don't… I'm literally bathing in my own piss right now. My catheter has burst.'

'I can leave if it's better for you, hun,' she replied awkwardly. I refused to be beaten and asked her to find me some help at the nurses' station and to hang around so we could catch up once I'd been cleaned.

It took a good ten minutes or so for the nurses to give me a full wash and change my gown and bedding, Katy waited patiently, and then we were able to catch up and have a chat. She was visiting a family member in another ward and had kindly swept by to catch up with me first and offered to help me with some leg exercises. Fantastic… a girl after my own heart. I am so thankful to her for helping me through that moment and other visits where she helped with exercises, supporting my recovery. I still have the many pairs of funky surgical bed socks she brought me!

Despite so many struggles, I somehow found the tolerance to push through and accept things far better than I had in the early days. I wasn't firing off every little frustration to Martin all day long or letting everything build up inside me. No, I started to take it moment by moment, letting each incident pass me by after it had happened. I made continued efforts with my daily gratitude diary, giving particular thanks to Hal and his video which had brought about this shift in my attitude, and leant heavily on meditation and other calming techniques.

However, I was not yet the grand master of calmness and I will never forget one hot day towards the end of August.

With the independence of raising my own bed, I was up and down like a yoyo one particular day because I kept getting the urge for a bowel movement. I could not bear the thought of people seeing my face should I need to pass a small poo; it was far safer to be down flat, either under my sheet or preferably out of sight with my curtains drawn around me. This particular day was a Saturday, I remember because it was carnival day in Cromer and Martin was maxed out with the chaos in the café. As it was a weekend, we had an agency nurse on duty whose persona I can only compare to that of Miss Trunchbull. I called her over with a look of urgency in my eyes and asked her to pull the curtain.

'Why?' she asked coldly

'Because I need to go.'

'Go where?'

Really? Was she that stupid? There was a bloody great big sign above my head saying "Spinal Patient" that I had insisted was put there for this very reason. I told Miss Trunchbull that I needed privacy to go for a poo and she kindly pulled the curtain around. I then heard Shirley complain to her. At this, she went off for a few minutes, obviously to get a second opinion on the matter, and then just as Pachelbel's "Canon" was reaching its climax in my headphones with me mid-push, she rudely yanked the curtains open around me, exposing me to the entire ward. I felt naked.

'I have to be able to see you at all times!' she snapped

I was horrified. 'What, even when I'm in the middle of having a poo?' I snapped back.

'Yes,' she growled at me, and carried on about her work. I sat there in complete shock, feeling humiliated and upset, too tense to finish what I'd started.

I phoned Martin in heaps of tears, but the crowds were flocking to Breakers for the outdoor BBQ stand that he had set up for the day. He was rushed off his feet and couldn't really speak to me, so I sent a long text for him to read later, ranting about what had happened. There was no amount of deep breathing that was going to relieve me of this one!

I pressed the buzzer and demanded to speak to someone from Mental Health, feeling unable to cope with my distress. This was only the second time in my entire hospital stay that I had called upon them.

As I went back down to my private place of lying flat, I pulled the sheet up around me and tried to calm my breathing, but the judders and little sobs were hard to get under control. How could a human being be so despicable? What made it worse was how she sauntered past me a couple of times and, despite seeing how upset I was, just glared at me. No sympathy or kind words and in fact, all she said to me was:

'Rules are rules,' with a satisfied look on her face.

Well, these hadn't been the bloody rules for the last six weeks, but I couldn't bring myself to confront her. I was too embarrassed and humiliated. I sensed Shirley's smugness that she had got her way, with the curtain now pulled back and not "suffocating" her space.

When Martin finally picked up my messages, he was horrified. He got straight on the phone to the ward sister and kicked off big time. 'Can you explain to me why someone who wants to use a bed-pan or commode gets the curtain pulled around them, and yet my wife who is forced to have to go in the bed does not get given the same level of privacy or respect for her dignity?'

Thankfully a wonderful ward sister came to see me as a result and sat holding my hand for half an hour whilst I blubbed and explained how stressful and difficult bowel movements were for me. How this had been the final straw. She initially tried to excuse Miss Trunchbull's behaviour and said that there may have been a miscommunication, that she had responded to Shirley's complaint and maybe hadn't realised that I was having a bowel movement. I assured her this wasn't the case because I had told her clearly to her face what I was doing.

The sister went off for five minutes to make some further enquiries. I imagined the evil Miss Trunchbull making her excuses, probably making up a pack of lies to cover her own back. They didn't work though, as the sister came back and assured me that she would be reported and never be put on our room for any care again should she continue at the hospital. Thank God for that.

I then pointed my finger towards the curtain sectioning me from Shirley, widening my eyes at the sister. I whispered that I couldn't take her complaining anymore and how she made me feel pressured and guilty for having my curtain drawn. The sister said she was aware there were tensions between us, and whilst not making any promises, there was another bed that had become available which she was doing her best to get me allocated to. This new bed was by a window in a different room, with a view. I was so excited; a change of scenery would be so good. I cancelled my visit from Mental Health as Sister had dealt with me so sensitively and had resolved what had been a shocking experience.

Thankfully things were on my side and I was on the move again, that very same evening too. I watched as nurses packed up my stuff around me, loading everything on top of me in the bed and then, after a very unconvincing 'Goodbye' to Shirley whom I got a fleeting glimpse of, I was wheeled round to a new room on the other side of the ward.

I was right by the window this time, with a tranquil view of green fields and trees just beyond the hospital perimeter. The sun was setting in the distance, and I felt sheer joy at the fact that I now had a view.

My new room was pretty much the same as the one before, with five other beds, only three of which were occupied at the moment. The familiar cringe-worthy cream and purple 1980s patterned curtains hung as the dull privacy dividers, a sink and two clinical waste bins stood in front of my bed and I had slightly more space around my bed, in the way new houses on the corner plot often have a little more space. I certainly felt I'd moved up a star rating, a trophy I felt was welldeserved.

One thing that was clearly not the same, was the missing clock on the wall above the surgical waste bins. I would have to use my watch or mobile to see how long until Martin would be with me again. He FaceTimed me a call with Mabel and Chester to cheer me up that evening, since he was too shattered to visit after carnival day. Chester ignored the screen as usual, whereas Mabel listened to everything I said, obeying my commands for treats being given by Martin and even barking at me when I asked her to "speak".

I took a deep breath before I settled down to sleep, listening to our wedding song, "Mr Blue Sky" as I drifted off, imagining the sand beneath my feet when we had got married on that beach in Antigua.

They say a change is good as a rest. This was definitely a good change and a good riddance to Shirley and Miss Trunchbull.

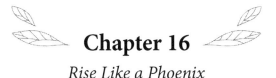

Chapter 16

Rise Like a Phoenix

As I raised my bed up each morning, I was greeted with the depressing picture of an old lady who seemed permanently asleep with her bed fixed at about twenty degrees. Her long dark hair was perched like a bird's nest on top of her head, her mouth seemingly frozen in a wide painful yawn set in her ghostly white face. She made me think of the Edvard Munch painting "The Scream" and looked like she was in pain as she snored away. She refused food or drink despite the nurse's emphatic attempts, and barely opened her eyes even when she had a visitor; it seemed as though she wanted to sleep and never wake up. So, I was surprised one morning to hear her clapping, and when I looked over, I realised she had been watching me. I had been trying to lasso my yoga strap onto my left foot to lift my leg a little higher than usual but had accidentally let the strap slip out of my hand mid-throw resulting in it landing out of my reach. I had to raise the back of my bed to nearly forty degrees where it took at least five minutes fumbling around with my extendable back scratcher to scoop it up like hook-a-duck at the fairground. Then, moving back to the hoopla stall, I was lobbing the strap time and time again until it finally caught my toes and I wriggled it onto my foot. Proud of my accomplishment, I looked up to see her smiling at me and gave a bemused smile back, glad that I had entertained her before she promptly fell back to sleep.

Having never spent a night in hospital other than having my tonsils removed as a child, I was certainly making up for lost time now, rising to the challenge by keeping myself busy each day. I listened to audiobooks on my phone (although I would often fall asleep and wake up having missed numerous chapters), I learnt how to do Sudoku (although for the life of me I have no idea why), I enjoyed crosswords and magazines but found it difficult to focus on reading books; I even found I had to re-read pages a number of times in Hal's book "The Miracle Equation".

My independence had greatly increased now that I was sitting up at 45 degrees: with the help of my back-scratcher I could reach for my phone charger plugged in behind me as well as reach magazines and other things on my table; I no longer had to call the nurse each time my phone slipped down the bed or my foot blocks moved out of place. I felt less of a burden on all of my carers. I looked forward to my visitors which also helped to pass the time (when my poop dilemma allowed). There were the girls who visited me from Mental Health, as well as friends and colleagues from Tropic. Life was almost enjoyable. As the famous quote by Darwin goes:

It is not the strongest of the species that survives, nor the most intelligent that survives. It is the one that is the most adaptable to change (Charles Darwin).

I was certainly surviving.

My two physio angels turned up to see me mid-morning with the news that they would be returning at lunchtime to help me sit on the edge of the bed for the first time; this gave me time to contact Martin who promised he would move heaven and earth to arrive on time.

I had bowel care and blood tests to get through first though and found myself yet again with tears pouring down my face as I was left to do the deed after enemas were put in. As I listened to Mozart's "Eine Kleine" on my headphones, I pictured myself sitting on the toilet in our little ensuite at home, looking out of the window over the expanse of our side garden and looking across the fields which stretch out to the tree-lined horizon. I would *never* take that view for granted ever again should I ever get back there. As soon as my curtain was drawn with the deed done, I snapped straight back to chirpiness; what went on behind the curtain stayed behind the curtain now.

Nurse Rachel popped in to say 'Hi' later on and to wish me luck. I was so excited, but also a tad nervous. I couldn't quite believe I was going to sit up today at last.

'Take it easy, Nik, don't overdo it, you're doing so well.'

Take it easy? I don't think so, not if that meant laying off my goal to take some steps by the end of the following week!

Can you truly imagine how it feels to have been flat for nearly five weeks? I mean you can't roll over and sleep on your side, you can't shuffle or wriggle to get comfortable, it is as if your back has been cemented to the bed. The only release had been when log rolled for a brief time before being planted back on the bed. I had no idea what to expect but had been told it may be a little painful, so my wimpiness accepted the healthy dose of morphine I was offered beforehand.

Martin came rushing through the curtain just in time; the girls and I were ready to go. As usual, it had taken him nearly an hour to find a parking spot. After picking Cathy up from the end of the bed to prevent her from getting caught or tangled, thus accidentally pulling (ouch!), the two ladies log-rolled me to face my right side. So far so good. Anna crouched near my knees and Emily was holding my shoulders, they now asked me to push myself up onto my elbow so they could swing me up to a sitting position. What? Now I was nervous.

'It will be fine, on the count of three,' Anna instructed. Martin winked at me.

'One, two, three...'

I groaned as I came up, probably a little over-dramatically as it really wasn't *that* painful. Then I was up, just sitting there, with Emily positioned behind me, holding my back and Anna supporting me from the front. Oh wow; as the blood rushed to my head, I focused on taking long, deep breaths. My legs were shaking, and it felt more than a little scary, but I was *not* going to ask to be put back down like Shirley had.

I had not been prepared for how alien everything felt. My body felt like a crushed bug, broken and frail, and I had no strength to hold myself up. The lack of core muscles meant my arms were fundamental in supporting me. Anna let go of me from the front and knelt down. Both girls kept reassuring me and asking if I wanted to lie back down. It was confusing and nothing like I had expected, but I was adamant I didn't want to lie back down. I had the 30 August imprinted in my mind.

Martin had tears streaming down his face, which in turn made me cry. How could sitting up to be such a momentous occasion in our life? Well, I suppose it was our first moment of real hope, a feeling that things were going to be okay… I was going to be okay.

Anna asked if I could shuffle a little closer to the edge of the bed and then put my foot on the floor. As I reached with my toe for the grey speckled linoleum, it felt like someone had cut my hamstrings; the stretch was even more intense than the first bed raise had been.

'Will this get easier each time I do it?' I asked, in desperate need of some reassurance.

'Yes, the first time is always the hardest, like it is with anything,' Anna said.

I briefly panicked that I was going to lose my balance.

'Are you still there, Emily?' She reassured me she was. I practised lifting one arm and then the other and soon felt brave enough for Emily to let go of me from behind whilst her hands remained poised to catch me if I wobbled back. Wow, despite having so little balance, I was doing it. I was sitting up by myself.

The view out of the window in front of me was of the car park below. Struggling to appear "fine" and a little self-conscious of all eyes being on me, I asked Martin to point out our car, the blue Volkswagen T-Roc which seemed part of a previous life. It was parked around the corner apparently. If I'm honest, I had to fake my interest in the conversation we all had, since it was all very overwhelming and I yearned to lie back down.

Five minutes later (which felt like half an hour), I was finally returned to the welcoming arms of my bed. Argh… bliss. Security and comfort resumed. Whilst I felt happy with my accomplishment it was tinged with fear of how much further there was to go; it was Friday and I only had one week to achieve my goal which seemed inconceivable to me right now.

Anna and Emily straightened me back up in bed and I told them about my goal; I'd decided I needed to get them on board.

'I know I'm being rather demanding here, but is there's any way on earth you can help me achieve this, please? It's so important to me and I've told the whole world I'm going to take steps before the end of August.'

Anna smiled at me and said they would do their best, but a lot depended on how well I adjusted to being upright and which physio staff were on shift. Apparently, I could only practise this with two physios and, as it was now the weekend, I wouldn't be sat up again until Monday now. That would mean only five days until the end of August.

'I'm so proud of you, darling, now you must get some rest.' Martin rushed back to the café and the chaos that had become his life.

A little later on, I browsed the photos Martin had taken of the event, unsure whether to share them on Facebook or not since the expression on my face made me look like I was giving birth; slightly panic-stricken with a ghostly complexion and hardly looking my best! I posted them anyway; it was a momentous part of my recovery and the beginning of the next phase where we would find out whether these legs of mine were going to work again or not. The comments of support were so heart-warming; it's amazing who pops out of the woodwork when word gets around that you're in hospital. Even the mayor of Cromer was commenting on my posts! I slept solidly for a few hours, as I was indeed exhausted.

Sherri, the spinal nurse, was so impressed when she heard about my progress that she immediately phoned Sheffield to update them. She felt I now needed to get there sooner rather than later, as did we all! Martin had an in-depth conversation with her as well as the mental health team to propose they put pressure on Sheffield to get me fast-tracked, emphasizing that it was detrimental to my mental health having to wait. I was only in fifth position, and he seemed to feel it would help push things on quicker if they were told about my psychotic episode. This felt a little wrong to me because I was in no more in need of mental health support than anyone else now. I was so focused on my physical recovery that it made me cringe to think that the first thing my new carers would learn about me was the fact that I had been mentally so unwell.

The last day of August was on Saturday, which meant I probably wouldn't have physio, and certainly wouldn't have *two* therapists. Therefore, I had to take my steps by Friday 30th. Even if it was just one step, I would be happy. Whilst I'm sure most people hadn't even remembered my Facebook post at the beginning of the month claiming I would take twenty steps by the end of August, and probably wouldn't care either way, *I* did. I would be failing myself if I didn't just take one!

Tuesday lunchtime, three days before D day: Anna and Emily arrived for physio. They brought with them some strange red contraption. It was a standing frame on wheels that looked a little like a sack barrow with a toe plate; the kind of monstrosity you would expect to see Hannibal Lecter attached to…

'We just brought it for you to see, so that *when* you're ready you know what we will use to stand you up with.' I wondered why I needed a preview of this monstrosity. We began the process of raising me up to sit on the side of the bed; this was my third time. It felt much easier already, less pain on the initial pull-up, and I was now able to shuffle myself a little better to the edge of the bed. As I sat there, tapping my feet and steadying my spinning head, I asked them why I couldn't try the standing frame right then.

'You can if you want,' Anna said. Bring it on…

'Get the camera ready!' I answered.

There was quite a build-up, similar to that of an athlete preparing on the starting blocks for his race. I was given a list of instructions on how to propel myself upwards and warned to prepare myself for how giddy I might feel once I got there.

I put my hands onto a section of the cold metal bars and took some deep breaths. The girls were supporting me from both sides and assured me they wouldn't let me fall. After a count of three, I groaned dramatically as I lunged forwards and, with some help from both girls, lifted up and onto the frame. For a split second I thought I wasn't going to make it. My legs were weak and shaky, like the muscle fatigue you get after an intense workout, but I felt secure now I was up. The girls both let go of me and I stood hanging on for dear life, my white knuckles gripping on to the metal bars. Anna took the obligatory photo.

'Has Shirley managed to stand yet?' I asked, secretly hoping that maybe I had overtaken her now. Neither of them answered me. Patient confidentiality of course.

After a minute of standing, I sat back down again. My strength had contributed to about 60% of the stand and I wanted to improve on this. We practised one more time; it took every ounce of strength I had but I did it. The girls told me I increased to around 80% of the lift this time. This was better and I felt hugely satisfied as I was lowered back down to my bed again. It's strange looking back how everything I was learning mirrors everything we learn as babies. Sitting up assisted, then unassisted, standing to hold on to furniture. I just prayed that I would be able to toddle again.

Wednesday, two days to D Day: Physio told me we would be doing the same today. We would stand with the Hannibal Lecter frame and the next day, practise wheeling me on it (like a sack of potatoes). Anna told me this was in preparation for wheeling me to the chair. The chair which was a whole two feet away from my bed. I was disappointed, to say the least.

'What? I don't want to sit,' I protested. Despite how tough this was, a great deal harder than I had first imagined, I had to try at some point, right? Why not now? I *had* to take those steps by Friday. The girls didn't reply, and I caught them looking at each other with a kind of *this one is really making my job difficult* look. I felt disheartened, realising that I was building my hopes up too much and was quite alone with my goal. It wasn't fair of me to put them under this amount of pressure; perhaps I would get them into trouble!

Thursday, one day to D Day: Anna wasn't with Emily today, and I was slightly disappointed. The red frame came again, along with a young Irish guy I'd not met before. Having got me into an upright stand again, they wheeled me around a little whilst I hung on. Now I do mean a little, since, despite having the *corner plot*, the space around my bed when the curtain was drawn was hardly playgroundsized; but moving around even a little gave me the sensation of movement and balance.

'Do you know if I'm having physio on Saturday?' I asked, aware that I was like that persistent child constantly whining to get their own way. They could not guarantee I would be slotted in and said it was totally out of their hands. I started to feel glad that I hadn't continued "bigging" up my intentions on social media to take those damn steps. It wasn't looking hopeful now.

FRIDAY, D-DAY: I secretly hoped it would be Anna and Emily coming together today, knowing it would be my last chance to take some steps and the pair of them knowing how much it meant to me. It felt like the longest morning of my life waiting for physio to arrive. Who was coming? I tried listening to my music but couldn't relax. I tried to do Sudoku, but my brain couldn't focus.

Lunch came and went. Then, finally, in marched Emily and Anna who started to pull my curtain around as usual. But hang on, no Hannibal Lecter frame or any other contraption! Damn… this meant we weren't going to be taking any steps. I tried to hide my disappointment and then… just as they prepared to roll me for my lift, a third physio opened the curtain and came in holding a walking frame. It one of those silver Zimmer frame thingies that old people use. YES! Today was the day! I squealed with excitement, but was equally panicked because Martin wasn't there.

'That's why Peter is here, to video it for you.'

They'd thought of everything.

Once perched on the edge of the bed with the frame in front of me, the girls assured me that it wasn't too different from the standing frame. I gripped the top of the flimsy silver frame, both girls either side again, this time with one leg on the bottom bar of the frame to keep it stable. Then, with their support under each arm, I was up. My hands were pressing down so hard that my knuckles were white with the strain and my arms trembling.

After clear instructions on what to do, I tentatively tried moving my right leg forward first, well, best foot forward, after all. It was a kind of shuffle, but it moved! Enough to be considered a step anyway. I then edged the frame forwards a little, before the left leg, which was far harder to feel, somehow shuffled enough to join alongside. After a few deep breaths, the girls asked me to step back towards the bed. My face on the video shows my disgust that they didn't let me try any more steps! I tentatively took the two fragile steps back again and sat down on the bed. Well, I had done it… I had taken two steps! I was shaking like a leaf.

After a drink of water and the girls checking I was okay, I was astonished that they allowed me to have another go. Yes! Cameraman to the ready… I stood up, and this time slowly took *two* steps forward and then back to the bed. I was shaking not only on the outside but on the inside now as well. As I sat back down on the bed I burst into tears. I was a weepy mess of relief. Even Emily and Anna had tears in their eyes; happy tears all round!

I think I may have told them both that I loved them as they lowered me back down and straightened me up. I was intoxicated with my success, buzzing with the anticipation of telling Martin and the world that I had done it. Anna and Emily showered me with praise and then admitted that they had had reservations about whether to go ahead or not, fearing I may not have been ready. I thanked them a thousand times before they left.

I sent Martin the video, and he replied almost instantly. 'I have tears streaming down my face right now. Nikki, you are fucking fantastic!'

As I lay there feeling proud enough to burst, I watched the playback of the video with which I was about to announce to the world that, albeit not the twenty I had promised, I *had* taken some steps. But then as I watched, I counted the steps: the first attempt had been one step forward with each foot, plus one step back again, so four in total. Then the second attempt was two steps forward and back with each foot… totalling eight steps. I made that a whopping twelve steps in total! Whilst I hadn't reached the full twenty that I had stipulated, I was certainly very happy with where I had landed. On the exact date that I had pledged… I had proven to the world and to myself that I was doing this, I was going to walk again. My favourite quote had never felt truer:

★*Aim for the moon, even if you miss you still land among the stars* ★

Chapter 17

Sheffield Here We Come!

Five days had passed since my first tentative steps, which I had proudly shared on Facebook. The world was cheering me on, and it felt great. Perhaps I was sensationalising my recovery a little, but it was driving me forwards and I knew I still had a long way to go.

I had managed on two more occasions to take a few steps with the Zimmer frame; in fact not only three or four steps forwards but also sideways like a crab! There was nowhere to go from here though; the limited space around my bed and lack of any further facilities made my move to Sheffield more urgent now. I had Googled pictures of rehab centres and seen the white parallel bars people use to learn to walk again. I was itching to get started, like a child awaiting their first day of school. I had even brought some fingerless leather gloves in preparation, a bit like the gloves that weightlifters wear, but with pink piping of course. These would stop friction burns with my wheelchair if I needed one. I had also invested in a matching pink and black bum bag to carry my phone in, and a new pink water bottle. Oh yes, I had all the gear: yoga straps, weights, water bottles, matching bum bag and gloves. I had given Martin endless lists of things to pack too, ready for when I would get the go-ahead for Sheffield.

We were now into September, with summer nearly over, and I was starting to feel like Sheffield was never going to happen. But like with everything, just when I had accepted that it was unlikely to happen anytime soon, as if by magic, it did.

Catriona, the sister on duty, was chatting with me in my "room" with the curtain drawn, when she casually dropped the words, 'seeing as you're off to Sheffield now...' into the conversation.

'What do you mean?' I interrupted.

'Didn't you know, you're off to Sheffield?' She looked confused, as if I should have known already.

'You're kidding, right? I'm still fifth, I can't be? No one's told me.'

Catriona looked a tad confused, convinced she had read it in my notes.

'Please go and double and triple check,' I begged, terrified to let myself believe this news for fear it might be wrong. She returned a few minutes later to confirm that, yes, I was being discharged and transport was being put in place to transfer me to Sheffield in two days' time. Still not convinced, Catriona phoned the discharge team and got someone to speak to me. The voice on the other end confirmed it was true. Hallelujah! I couldn't believe my luck. How could I have waited seven weeks to move up the queue only two places and then suddenly spring to first place like this?

Sherri confirmed things the following day. I found myself thinking of Shirley again and asked if she was already there since she had been further up the queue than me. Sherri side-stepped my question. However, another nurse did let slip that Shirley had gone off to Cambridge to a private rehab centre, not a specialist spinal unit though; she was still waiting to be transferred to Sheffield from there. It was never said in so many words, but it seemed that telling them about my mental health issues had done the trick. It was finally happening.

Martin arrived laden with bags for our mission of packing and sorting. I had accumulated so much clutter, and hadn't been able to tidy or keep on top of it, for obvious reasons. First, he had a grey holdall to pack everything in that needed to be taken back home. He took down all the cards from the shelf behind me. I would read these all properly when I got home, I decided. Then he swept along the window shelf scooping up books, baskets, magazines and boxes of chocolates; I told him to take them all! Then we went through the magician's cupboard to the side of me… it had different hidden doors to get into it from every side. There were Sudoku books, which I doubted I would have time for in Sheffield, numerous pairs of surgical socks and an array of other items… it all had to go. Out came the slipper socks, wait… they needed to be packed for Sheffield; ever prepared, I had ordered these from Amazon thinking I may need some non-slip socks for walking around in (pah!). I'd also ordered myself some fancy new trainers and leisurewear. Oh, I laugh as I type this back, I think Margo thought she was off to a five-star pampering retreat with a jacuzzi and spa, she had no idea what was coming! Next, all the Tropic products were pulled out of the magic cupboard, in their neatly labelled bags. These were packed in a small case that was coming with me on my journey the next day. I almost had the excitement you get when packing for a proper holiday, but I guess things are relative; anything was going to feel exciting having been chained to this bed for the last seven weeks.

Next, Martin went through the case of clothes he had brought me to take. Note to all women, *never* ask a man to pack for you, no matter where you are going. He had packed enough clothes for a month's excursion to the Himalayas, including fleeces, jumpers and jackets.

'Apparently, it's *hot* on the ward there…' I protested, arguing with him to take some of them back.

'Well, there's no harm in taking a few warmer clothes. What if you go outdoors?' he said, ignoring me and putting them back in the case. He then proceeded to pull out some ridiculous items that I pleaded with him to take back.

'I just need comfy clothes,' I groaned. Sherri had said I would only need leggings or trackie bottoms (for easy access to my catheter) and t-shirts; long or short-sleeved.

'Have you brought the deliveries that came for me?'

'Yes,' he answered and pulled out an unopened Next bag and M&S bag which had my new size 12 comfy clothing in; I felt confident that I had gone down two dress sizes. The thought of wearing clothes was really exciting after being in these hideous hospital gowns for what seemed like an eternity now; they really do de-humanise you after a while.

I made Martin promise to FaceTime me with the doggies before he went to sleep that night, feeling like the distance to Sheffield would make me miss them more than ever. I also gave him a list of things he had forgotten (like my laptop) so he could bring them when he came up to see me in Sheffield at the weekend, and we said our goodbyes.

Words can barely describe the mix of excitement and nerves I felt, knowing I was off to *boot camp* as the nurses had called it. Bring it on! I wanted the opportunity to push for new goals and further my road to recovery. Yes, there was a little fear too. Fear of the unknown of where I was going and how long for. Fear of the uncertainty of how much mobility I would regain and whether or not I would get back to a life that resembled anything like it had been before this had happened. But I was desperate to get back to my doggies, and I now understood Sheffield was the place to make it happen. The excitement was so great I couldn't sleep that night; I felt like a child who was going on a trip to Disneyworld.

The following morning was to be my last at the N&N. I was so overwhelmed with how many nurses came to say goodbye to me. I had obviously become a familiar part of the furniture in the place; an instantly recognisable face for them as they came on shift. I was an emotional wreck; this had been my home for the past seven weeks, a place that I had learnt to find some comfort despite the struggles, but now I was off to "big school".

'Make sure you come back and see us when you're whizzing around in that wheelchair!'

'Er… no; I'll be back here on my crutches chasing you down the corridor!' I laughed.

Rachel gave me the biggest hug and I told her I would miss her awful singing. I would always remember how she cheered the ward up playing tracks from her mobile phone. I had requested Queen and she'd had us all stamping and clapping along to "We Will Rock You". Well, some of us not stamping, obviously.

Sherri gave me some final details and advised me to have some morphine before I set off to make the journey more comfortable. This was fine with me… I was growing quite fond of the magical sweet stuff. She also told me that my catheter would be left unclipped on free flow, which I was relieved about as I didn't want any wee "detours" on the way up there, or worse still another bladder contraction. I had had tests done, and a new catheter put in (ouch!) to try to resolve the dreaded bladder spasms that had begun, but nothing showed up, no signs of a UTI or anything else, so it remained a mystery. I had a quiet word with my lady minions, telling them that if my catheter were to be taken out permanently, they would get to have a big 'ole party with their husbands from the bowel department. So please work on it!

My transport arrived later that morning, with the driver and an assistant who would be accompanying me in the back. He reminded me a bit of Jimmy Nail and had a welcoming northern accent. However, I was soon to discover he was *not* particularly friendly: not rude or unhelpful, but merely "uninterested", it seemed.

Once I had been transferred onto the portable trolley and strapped in, all my bags were balanced on top of me with a nurse following behind with my excess baggage.

I was ceremoniously wheeled out of Gately Ward with the nurses all wishing me luck as I passed them. The emotion

I felt as I went past the nurses' station was overwhelming and tears were pouring down my face. I had realised I would feel like this, believing I would be well rid of the place. I somehow knew though, that I would be coming back to pay a visit when my ordeal was finally over.

As Gately faded to the distance, I was wheeled through the bright corridors of the hospital and down towards the exit, feeling every bump in my fragile back which seemed as though it were made of glass.

Daylight and fresh air were a new welcome sensation; it felt a bit like stepping outside of an aeroplane after a very long flight. I embraced the cool breeze sweeping along my face and tousling my overgrown hair. The sunshine was the best bit. I closed my eyes and craned my neck to feel its warm rays on my face. Sometimes you don't realise how much you miss something until you get it back. I asked the transport guys to allow me a couple of moments before putting me in the back of the vehicle. Tears again. I needed to get a grip!

I was strapped into the van facing the rear doors, so hoped this wouldn't make me feel travel sick. Jimmy Nail strapped himself next to me and I asked how long he thought the journey would take.

'Depends on traffic, but I would say around three and a half, possibly four hours.' That was pretty much the extent of our interaction and the last thing he said to me since he made it quite clear he wasn't up for a chatty journey and kept his head stuck in his iPad. Rude!

As we set off, I gripped the bars tightly on the side of the trolley as every movement was exaggerated in my over-sensitive spine. I wasn't broken in very gently; we went over some speed bumps as we left the hospital grounds and the look of horror on my face managed to force a reassuring smile from Jimmy Nail. I had not anticipated this; it felt like my back could shatter at any moment and every roundabout or twist in the road had me clinging on to the sides like it was a white-knuckle ride. Thank god Sherri had made me have some morphine.

After about half an hour I started to settle and relax into the ride a little but had a nagging sensation like I was going to have a bladder spasm. I asked Jimmy to check my pee bag, and sure enough, the nurses had forgotten to leave it on free flow. He switched this for me, then went back to his iPad, slightly irritated by the interruption. I decided to put my headphones on, and Elton John kept me company for the remainder of the journey. Like always, my emotions were stirred with the music and as I watched the Norfolk countryside flash past my eyes the enormity of my injury sank in a little more. I had broken my spine and I was starting my journey back out into the world now. I felt a mix of trepidation and gratitude.

My geography and in fact history are both very poor, but the scenery started to change some hours later. As I saw the drab grey buildings start to emerge, and we passed what looked like old disused steel factories, I had a sneaking suspicion we must be close.

We pulled into The Northern General Hospital, the speed bumps confirming our arrival, and weaved through the endless departments on the hospital site before descending a steep slope towards the Spinal Unit. I felt butterflies in my tummy. Jimmy and the driver wheeled me out into the cold crisp evening air and into a smallish-sized building that looked like an office block from the outside. We went up in a lift to floor one (I noticed there were only two floors) and I was delivered to Osborne Ward.

'Hi, Nicola, I'm Connor.' I was greeted by a young self-assured lad whose accent made me think of *Calendar Girls* and "plum jam". I had once painstakingly practised this accent to audition for the role of "Chris" (played by Helen Mirren in the film) in our amateur dramatic society.

'I hadn't realised you would have a different accent here,' I said, immediately kicking myself for letting this be the first stupid thing to come out of my mouth, thus introducing Margo to my new carers.

'We're all like it up here.' He smiled, helping with the slide board transfer to get me on my new bed so that the transport drivers could set off with their trolley once more.

I was left for a short while, giving me time to take in my new surroundings. I was in a double room with a dividing curtain but the bed next to me was unoccupied. Good grief; a private room just for me, result! The glass partition to the right of me looked straight out onto the nurses' station/reception area which was quite reassuring. There were large windows to my left which would probably make the room bright in the morning. In addition to my bedside cabinet, I now had a double wardrobe and a set of plastic drawers too. It was significantly more spacious than the N&N but also more dated, verging on funky.

As I glanced around, waiting for someone to come and see me, I discovered a pull-down TV that was perched just above me, which I was soon to learn was free of charge. I had never bothered with the TV at the N&N, refusing their extortionate price for such a standard pastime.

'Honestly, it feels like a four-star hotel after the N&N,' I told Martin when I called to let him know of my safe arrival. 'I've got a room all to myself, and even a TV!'

Connor came into my room with his partner in crime, Sandra. I noticed she wore a lilac uniform instead of the blue that I was used to, adding to my sense of being in a foreign land. They were both going to log roll me to get me changed for the evening. Well, get me out of the trackie bottoms and sweatshirt that I was wearing and into my pyjamas. No clinical gowns here… it felt liberating.

Now I had been forewarned that I may be kept in a flat position in bed again, just until I was assessed and approved by the doctors here, but nobody had prepared me for what happened next.

'Roll yourself to the right,' Connor said. Huh?

'Oh no, I need to have four people log roll me,' I said, sounding like Margo again. I was scared that they didn't realise how fragile I was.

'Er no, it's been over seven weeks since your op now, love, you're fully healed and perfectly safe to roll.' Well, this was a shock. But this was a specialist unit dealing only with injuries such as mine so I had to trust them a little. He helped me to grip the cot sides and, with effort, I managed to pull myself over so he could check my back and undo my bra hooks. Wow, things were very different here.

'Do you want a hand with these?' Connor asked as he passed me my pyjamas. Well, today was the first time in seven weeks that I had worn any normal clothes, let alone dressed myself.

'I can do my top but that's about it,' I said feebly, feeling a little inadequate suddenly.

'Okay, we will help you, Nicola, but let's make it quite clear, within a few days we expect you to be doing as much for yourself as you can. Now is that the name you want us to call you, Nicola?

'I prefer Nikki if that's okay,' I said, my confidence rapidly slipping down the drain. They must have thought me some precious princess expecting them to handle me like glass. Perhaps there was a hidden pea under my orthopaedic mattress! Princess or not, this was not to be a very gentle introduction to my new home. In the N&N nurses had tentatively lifted my legs no higher than a few inches off the bed when changing my socks, by contrast, Connor and Sandra proceeded to yank my legs so high I thought I was doing the Can-Can. I yelped.

'Ooh, sorry,' they said and calmed things down a little. I started to worry that this may be some sort of initiation test. If it was, I was failing miserably.

Once changed into pyjamas I asked where my "pad" was in the bed.

'Oh, we don't believe in giving you nappies here.'

I dumbly asked the obvious.

'We give bowel care at six a.m. and you shouldn't need anything else in between, besides you will be up and about in your wheelchair.' Little did I know that the bowel care here was so efficient that my bowel issues were finally going to be over.

A young girl came in to measure my hips for my wheelchair.

'Do I have to have a wheelchair?' I asked, again realising as soon as it came out of my mouth that I sounded like Margo.

'How else will you get yourself to physio?' came the reply. Good point.

My wheelchair arrived an hour or so later and was left parked next to my bed for the following day. I looked it up and down. I looked away, almost pretending it wasn't there, and then I looked at it again. I could feel tears sting my eyes. Why did I need a wheelchair? I wanted to walk. I bit my lip as I looked at it with disgust, feeling it would be a step backwards if I were to get in it. Oh, how wrong I was. How I misjudged the wheelchair and its role in my recovery.

Chapter 18

Settling In

I awoke on my first morning at Sheffield, to the beautiful sound of the dawn chorus. I hadn't heard birds for so long. I felt a sense of "coming home" after a long time away and tears began rolling down my face. It is quite bizarre how I was moved to tears at this since I've never been deeply connected to nature in that way, not like Martin is. Well, I mean I love my country walks with the dogs, but I've never been one to stop and smell the roses. I pondered how this entire experience may be changing me.

I met Karen at breakfast time, a nurse whom I was to grow very fond of. She was probably in her late fifties, with waist-length wavy hair that was swept up into one of those claw-type hair grips allowing it to cascade over the top in a ponytail. She was quite petite and a slightly older and more northern version of myself I thought; a little feisty and liked a "laff". The northern accent definitely played a part in making everyone seem so welcoming and down to earth. Karen was especially kind, and spent longer with me than any other nurse, giving me extra reassurance and support. It seemed she took pity on my naivety and would give me the heads up or top tips, making me feel like we were on the same team and in this together.

She brought me my first breakfast which was a plate of hot tinned tomatoes with bacon and toast. Luxury. It felt like a Michelin star meal after the N&N slop I had grown used to. Now don't get me wrong, it was still very basic, but it was *hot,* and it was different. Every day was to be a hot breakfast with a choice of sausages, omelette, baked beans and bacon. I already felt my appetite coming back. My expression told Karen to take the Tommy Tippee cup away and bring me my mint tea in a mug, *without* a straw thank you very much!

'We'll be coming to give you a nice shower after your breakfast,' she said as she bounced out of the room. A shower? Nearly eight weeks with no shower or bath and yet somehow, it was about to happen? I felt confused, how could this be made possible and why had it never happened at the N&N? It soon became clear. I was transferred via a slide board to a dark blue waterproof trolley bed which had raised sides all the way around, turning it into some kind of bath on wheels. I was assisted with getting undressed and then, with just a flimsy towel to cover my femininity, was wheeled into a large clinical-looking wet room with a shower.

Karen checked the temperature was okay for me and then aimed the showerhead so that the water started to pour over my body; it was heavenly. The water was warm and comforting, almost reassuring my body that it was still there for me to reclaim. I hadn't even realised how much I had yearned for this; again being welcomed with a feeling of coming home. Karen gave me the shower and asked me to hold it over my upper body, whilst she made a start on washing my legs with my Tropic body wash. She commented on how good it smelt but then paused when she saw I had tears cascading down my face, merging with the shower water. I let it go and began to sob…

'It's okay, most people cry in their first shower, it's quite normal,' she said with a reassuring smile. I made a pact with myself that I would *never* take *having a shower* for granted again… I pictured myself standing in our little shower in the ensuite off our bedroom; when I was home, I would savour every drop of water and stand (or at the very least sit) and wash my body from head to toe, remembering this moment.

I liked it here already. I was liking these new experiences which were making me feel a step closer to home. Karen and Connor wheeled me back to my room to get dressed and we chatted freely, getting to know each other. Connor tried to familiarise me with the place, telling me reassuring stories about others like me and Karen said that in a couple of months when I was discharged, I would possibly find myself not wanting to go home. But hang on a moment… rewind:

'Oh, I'm not here for *months*,' I proudly announced. They both looked at me. 'I'm a bit hung up on goals and all that, and I'm planning to be out by the end of September; I've got to get home to my dogs.' I gave them my biggest smile. They both looked across at each other and then Connor broke it to me as they started to get me dressed.

'I can see you have some movement in your legs, Nikki, but realistically you will be here at least eight weeks, most people are here three to four months, and some are here up to eighteen months.' It was like a bucket of icy cold water. I froze, tight-lipped, whilst trying to absorb this information. You may as well have just told me I wasn't going to get my legs back, that I would never walk again. I could *not* be in here for months; why had no one told me? I felt like I had been tricked, duped into coming here. I had set my goal to be home by the end of September, which was a compromise in my world; a month longer than I had first anticipated. My lip wobbled as I tried my best not to show just how upset I was.

I blubbed down the phone to Martin, who didn't seem surprised at the news, and told me it was best to make the most of it here and get myself to maximum recovery. But I didn't want to accept it. My dogs would forget me, for God's sake. They needed their mum. I needed to get back to my business and my team of girls too. Nobody seemed to have the same sense of urgency or have any sense of belief in my goal-setting skills!

After spending about an hour and a half in X-ray having my spine examined from every angle, a doctor arrived to assess my movement and check for sensation. I wasn't asked to sit up or attempt walking, but merely to lift each leg and bend the knee just like my physio exercises. After the assessment, I was given a score on something called the Asia Scale: I was D2 apparently, on a scale that runs from A to E and 1 to 5; with A1 being the worse score. My school report was satisfactory; the first time in my life that a D was a positive result. It showed I had some motor and sensory function.

Connor came to have a chat with me about my injury and to find out how much I knew, which wasn't much, it seemed. There were to be group talks I could attend for an array of information from weight management to preventing pressure sores. Then there were lessons in wheelchair skills, and other activities to take part in. God, this was serious stuff. I was slightly overwhelmed that this was my life now but it was clear there was no way back and the sooner I embraced things the better. I asked Connor about "walkers" and he told me that yes, they did have *a few* patients who walked out of the hospital when discharged, but not many. He then did something to cheer me up (probably because he knew I was so upset at hearing I would be in here for months). He brought a patient to meet me: a mature man probably in his early sixties who was just using a walking stick. He stood there perfectly balanced whilst chatting to me, waiting to leave once his wife arrived to collect him. I sat there watching him in amazement; you could barely see he had an injury, the only thing giving it away was the stick. I surveyed him up and down and craned my neck, watching as he walked away. Yes, that would be me, I decided. He had only been here three weeks too, this pleased me even more.

Connor enjoyed sharing his years of acquired knowledge; I listened half-heartedly as he explained how the spinal cord has over twenty million nerves and that every injury is different, with no two people ever the same. I smiled in the right places and pretended to listen, but the truth was I didn't want to hear these details.

'Don't worry, you'll be an expert on spinal injuries by the time you leave us,' he laughed, obviously finding my perplexed look amusing.

Next, a very special someone was wheeled into my room, someone that would have such a meaningful impact on me and my life in the future which I didn't know yet. His name was Danny. Karen had asked him to come and reassure me about what being in a wheelchair was like since he had been using his for about a week. Despite his bikerish beard and long black hair, it struck me what a kind and gentle person Danny was. He emanated warmth with his smile and gentle voice as he spoke to me. He seemed a little timid, and I noticed his dark brown eyes which seemed to be hiding the most extraordinary amount of pain.

'It's fine, love, honest,' he said with his northern lull and a maturity that seemed way beyond his years. 'Just make sure you drink plenty of water as it helps you not to feel dizzy. You will get tired at first though.' Danny went on to tell me how he had been in a head-on collision with a tree which had got him into this mess. He had a few broken vertebrae as well as breaking both his arms; I noticed they were both covered in scars from all the surgery he had had. He had been in a coma for the first few weeks and was lucky to be here having nearly died, twice! Wow. It made me feel immediately grateful for my injury; I could see that it could have been so much worse. I felt rude when I couldn't reply to Danny's question.

'How d'ya do yours?'

I stammered, looking around for someone to help me out. Connor and Karen didn't jump to my rescue and I wondered if they even knew.

'It's okay, you don't have to tell me,' Danny said. I didn't. But I felt that awkward, gaping moment again. I needed to address this… and soon.

Martin bumbled into my room a few hours later, impressed with my new surroundings, and set about putting all my things in the wardrobe and bedside cabinet for me. How the heck would I ever get things out? I had clothes hanging in my wardrobe but how would I reach them?

'Is that your new wheelchair?' he said with a beaming smile, like it was a new BMW or something.

'Yeah, don't get used to it… it's not staying.' I must have sounded like a spoilt child who had been given an unwanted toy for Christmas.

Karen soon arrived with a hoist to lift me off the bed and get me into my new set of wheels. Now, this wasn't the most glamourous of events; the sling-type contraption squished me up like a crushed bug and hoisted me, with my limbs dangling over the edge, to the waiting wheelchair. I found it totally humiliating and uncomfortable with my tender injury plus I was fearful that I may wet myself. Martin started to snigger and asked if he could film the moment for Facebook. My answer was too blue to write.

Luckily the hoist didn't break down midtransfer, and there were no toilet accidents; I arrived safely into the wheelchair.

'As soon as you're signed off with the transfer board, you won't need this hoist,' Karen said as she put it all away. So, here I was in a wheelchair. Another first. For the life of me, I don't know what I had been expecting but it wasn't this. It hurt. Every muscle of my body ached with the effort of holding me up. It hurt to put my arm over the side to reach for the wheels, it hurt to lean forwards or backwards, it hurt to breathe. My body was a stranger to me again.

Karen reassured me that all my core muscles would build back up again with time; she reassured me I should persevere since if I asked to be lifted back into bed, I would have to stay there until the following day. That was the rule apparently, when using the hoist anyway. Seemed a bit harsh, but I guess it was to try to prevent patients from taking the easy option of getting back into bed; something that was screaming inside of me right now.

Martin was suddenly the expert on wheelchair skills and was trying to be helpful with his barrage of instructions on how to reverse, manoeuvre and steer. I resisted the urge to yell, 'Shut up.' Instead, I tentatively wheeled it forwards, a little surprised by how un-coordinated I was since I'd always been really good at all things "driving", especially those games and simulators you find in arcades. It didn't seem to help with this though; despite usually picking things up quickly, I could see this was going to need a little practise.

Martin took a photo of me and it took all my effort to smile, my eyes telling the true story. I didn't like this, and it wasn't long before I complained to Martin that I wanted to get back into bed.

'Nikki, you've got to persevere. You heard what Karen said… that unless you can build up to staying in it for four hours, they won't consider moving you up to Osborne 3.' God, if this place was big school, then when you passed the next test (probably being pottytrained and walking by holding on to furniture) Osborne 3 must be 6th form. I learnt that it was where patients gained further independence, preparing them for discharge and a clear sign of getting ready to leave. My ward was Osborne 1 and I would hopefully bypass Osborne 2, since this apparently was for people with bedsores. The thought of four hours in the wheelchair was more than painful; I didn't feel I could do four minutes right now. Osborne 3 felt a million miles away.

Martin pushed me slowly up a ramp and through double doors to an outside patio area with chairs and table and a non-spectacular view over a car park. Martin plonked himself down, talking enthusiastically, but I couldn't focus, my body was still screaming at me. I couldn't understand why it felt so uncomfortable and was fearful of just how difficult this journey was going to be, and then it happened… a sudden clamping feeling in my private parts which overwhelmed me and put me in a blind panic. It was a bit like a labour contraction, increasing in intensity, building to a crescendo with me fighting for breath. Thirty seconds later it was over, and I was crying. I insisted Martin go and get a nurse.

Karen rushed to my side and checked the catheter bag (attached to my leg) which had the tap closed since I was back on bladder training. It didn't appear that anything was wrong so she couldn't understand. She released the valve and let some urine out.

'Nothing to worry about, love, just release the valve if you feel you need to,' she said, matter-of-factly, and was gone.

Now I was miserable as hell. Martin couldn't seem to understand why I wasn't a little happier with my newfound freedom, pushing me for conversation. But my internal battle with fear was taking up all my thought space.

Somehow, I managed to last a full hour before I was hoisted back into my bed; god, what a relief it was. Security and comfort resumed. I glared at the wheelchair; well, I decided that had most definitely been a *fail*. Everyone was kind and told me how well I had done to last an hour on my first attempt; Connor warned me to be prepared for "banding" pain, something most patients get in the early days once back in bed. Oh yes, I experienced it alright; I would describe it as a rubber band being squeezed around my midriff at the exact height of the injury level. The clamping pain is caused by the core muscles coming back to life and I was reassured it would get easier. When I asked for some morphine, my go-to pain relief, the meds nurse asked me if I had had any codeine. When I said no, she said they preferred patients to take that before having morphine. Mmm, maybe not *everything* here was better than the N&N; there was a meds ranking system and morphine seemed to be at the top of the ladder! Thankfully, they succumbed later that evening when I could hardly breathe with the vice-like grip. The codeine hadn't touched the pain, but morphine helped a little more and relaxed me too.

After a delicious meal of hunter's chicken and mashed potato, I settled down to the luxury of some TV time, feeling more exhausted than ever before in my life. As I thought about how hard it had been today, I remembered Anna from physio telling me the first time I'd sat on the edge of the bed how the first time is always the hardest. Tomorrow was another day. It would be easier; it *had* to be.

Chapter 19
Wheels of Fire

I met the head of the physio team the next morning; Gary came to explain to me how my programme would work. I had been assigned my own personal trainer (well, physiotherapist) and my weekly timetable would be put up on my wardrobe door complete with my OT and physio time slots plus any other activities taking place that week. I was instructed by Connor that I was to take full responsibility for everything on the timetable and get myself to where I needed to be. Whilst the talks and other extra-curricular items were optional, attendance at physio and OT were not. I was advised that the more things I got involved with, the quicker I would be released. No one had warned me there would be extra-curricular police here!

After my assessment from physio, various doctors came in to speak to me and by the time my OT therapist popped into my room, my head was spinning. She was called Flo and was an upbeat and happy character; I liked her instantly.

'What exactly *is* OT?' I asked as Margo escaped from me again, but Martin had told me they would teach me to make a cup of tea and stuff. Bloody ridiculous, there was nothing wrong with my brain! Flo went into more detail, and I gradually started to open up to the idea. I appreciated that there could be difficulties I may encounter doing home chores, even if I wasn't in a wheelchair. I momentarily imagined the dilemmas from a wheelchair. I didn't want height adjusted worksurfaces or doors widened; I was going to be up on my feet!

Now first off, Flo wanted to help me get signed off for wheelchair transfer which would make life so much easier with the hoist redundant and giving me a little independence. Yet again, Martin arrived just in the nick of time for my performance. Using what I can best describe as a large skateboard without wheels, this piece of wood was used to help bridge the gap between my bed and the wheelchair. I pulled myself up to a sitting position on the edge of my bed, without any assistance. Wow, the first time I'd done that. Then I lowered the bed down to the same level as the wheelchair and bit by bit shuffled my bum onto the board and, using all my arm strength, managed to shuffle along it to get into the wheelchair. Success! The board was left behind on the bed for my return.

Flo then talked me through a list of instructions for positioning the wheelchair safely for all transfers. I was dazzled; surely it needed a manual like the one kept in a glove compartment? Release the catch and lift the arm up, make sure the brake is engaged on both sides with its handle folded down (in case it accidentally got stuck up your bum mid-shift), make sure the wheels are locked in a position facing forwards on the chair, release the footplates... Good grief! Mirror, indicate, manoeuvre! Was there to be an exam on all this stuff? Maybe my brain had just become too addled from sitting around in the N&N for so long. Martin had hinted as much, saying that I had become a tad institutionalized.

Flo said she would do one more transfer with me tomorrow and then sign me off, meaning I would have the freedom to get in and out of bed on my own whenever I wanted. She left, and I was alone with Martin. But damn! I was back in the wheelchair again and it *still* hurt.

I tentatively wheeled around my room, bumping into anything that got in my way and getting tangled up in the dividing curtain. My look of dismay told Martin not to give me any advice, so he started busying himself with organising stuff in my room. He came across my schedule pinned on the wardrobe door and took great delight in reading my school timetable out to me. I snapped his head off. Now I did immediately apologise, totally aware of my unreasonable mood, but I had such a tightness in my chest, tension like I have never experienced before. The anxiety was so great, I was barely breathing; it was as if I had just ventured into an icy cold sea and was trying to acclimatize myself. If I were going to get the hang of this wheelchair, this was the first thing I needed to address.

Lunch arrived about ten minutes later and I discovered it really hurt to learn forwards to reach my food.

'Can I have the tray on my lap?' I asked sheepishly. I knew I was being pathetic, but this was so scary, and I had never expected it to hurt quite so much.

'No, you can't.' Connor was smirking at my predicament. Was it my imagination or did he move the things on my trolley table slightly further out of my reach? Was this another initiation test?

'Can you pass me my drink?'

'No, you can do that, reach…' He laughed again, definitely mocking me.

Okay, I could see why this was called boot camp now. I could see that I was going to have to grow up and find a way through this. I had one mouthful of my lunch but was too anxious to eat any more. Martin tried to encourage me, but he had no idea how this felt, how could he? All I wanted was to get back into bed; I couldn't do this.

Martin was having a chat with Karen, laughing as they discussed what knickers he should buy me in M&S. He had packed me some black lacy ones, which weren't appropriate. Honestly, what was he thinking? Karen explained how the lace could cause pressure sores when sitting in the wheelchair, so he was instructed to go and get some large, plain *Bridget Jones* style ones.

'Try and be in a better mood when I get back,' he said, giving me one of his reprimanding looks.

I knew I wasn't being much fun, but he had no idea just how difficult this was. I burst into tears which led to the full flood gates opening. I poured out how exhausted I was, and that I just wanted to be back in my bed and how I was also scared of having another bladder spasm. This was all just so awful. I wallowed in my pity party, but not for long; Martin was going to give me some well-needed tough love. He told me that the choice was mine, that I could get back into bed if I wanted to, but it would be heading in completely the wrong direction for my recovery. He reminded me of the need to get to Osborne 3 and questioned how could I ever expect to reach my goal or progress if I started going backwards?

'You need to dig deep, Nikki, don't give in to this. You can do it; just find a little more willpower each day to do a little longer than the day before.' He gave me a big hug once my lecture had finished and then, after promising to be back in an hour or so with my new 'big girl pants', he was gone.

I looked at the bed, debating what I should do. Then I looked up at the clock. I hadn't even done one hour yet. I wheeled around to my bedside table and picked up my headphones and mobile phone. First off, I was going to listen to some relaxing music and do some work on my breathing. Then I would take it from there. Baby steps.

The soothing voice talked me through a meditation, starting with my toes and working through to my head, focusing on releasing the tension in every muscle, breathing in positivity and belief, breathing out all tension and discomfort. As I began to focus, I embraced what my body was feeling and breathed straight through the middle of it, willing my mind to find strength. It worked. After ten minutes of deep breathing, I was already feeling better. I saved the programme, knowing I would need it again. I wheeled over to pick up my pink padded headphones, found my favourite playlist, which was heavy rock, then I put on my "go faster" pink and black leather gloves and started wheeling myself out of my room. I was feeling braver, going on a bear hunt possibly. I pushed myself up the corridor past the nurses' station on the corner, slowly at first, to get used to the huge wheels and learning how to alternate pulling and pushing them to turn.

As the Rolling Stones started playing, my jaw tightened, and I increased my speed. Grey speckled lino lay ahead of me with two closed heavy wooden swing doors at the end. I pulled back on the wheels and skidded to a halt as I reached them. I briefly noticed a disused room as I spun myself around to head back. About thirty metres of corridor lay ahead of me with the ramp up to the outside patio at the end. The walls were a non-descript magnolia colour, with bluish-grey wide dado rails streamlining the route. I pushed myself with urgency; teeth gritted, I was building up some speed now, completely oblivious to the patients in the rooms on either side of the corridor. I just wheeled past, focusing on the damn chair. Heart pounding, I was going to beat it, I was doing this thing whether it hurt or not. I was halfway up the ramp when I came to a grinding halt, threatening to roll back as I gripped the wheels as hard as I could— thankfully Karen magically appeared from behind to finish pushing me up the last bit.

'A bit optimistic on your first day, madam,' she laughed.

Outside I had space to really practise my manoeuvres, big square patio paving slabs with just the odd potted plant dotted here and there. A low wall with black railings guarded the perimeter. Without anyone watching me and the freedom to grunt as much as I needed, I spent ten minutes giving myself a crash course on wheelchair skills. Then, I was ready to wheel myself back down the ramp, without a thought or care if I crashed at the bottom; I was *doing* this. Well, not only did I manage to wheel down the ramp, but I did a cool left slide at the bottom, kind of like a handbrake turn, before setting off down the other side of the corridor towards the lifts. A couple of nurses at the station peered up as I passed them, then smiled at each other. Each track was pumping me on, as

I pushed, turned and manoeuvred myself around. God, I love rock music.

Karen came and found me wheelchair dancing down the end of the corridor and took me for a spin around the ward. We did an entire circuit and she pointed out Osborne 2 ward, and Osborne 3. The whole place was like a throwback from the seventies, in desperate need of modernisation but all adequately suited for its needs. The dining room had a corner area with a pool table, neighboured by a glass-enclosed library with automatic doors. We went in so that Karen could show me the resident fish in their oversized tank and a children's play area with toys and books. I was introduced to an elderly lady sitting at a table in her wheelchair. She looked relaxed, comfortable in the chair, which gave me hope.

Back in the dining room, there were about eight tables. It was a self-service canteen with a hot food bar and a coffee machine at the end. Apparently, Osborne 3 patients were independent enough to come and use this café on their own. I found myself wondering how they managed to carry a tray with food and wheel themselves to the table. I guessed things like this would become clear, and decided not to worry for now since I would continue having my food in my room. Karen explained that we were allowed to eat in here with our friends or family members and order takeaways in too. Wow, privileges! This place was so cool. Or at least it would be when I got the hang of this discomfort and anxiety.

All three of the Osborne units wove around in a large circle ending up back in our ward. Before returning we paused at some large scales which Karen pushed me on to get my weight. She knew the exact weight of the wheelchair to subtract. It appeared I had lost two stone! Wow— I hadn't been this weight since before having my girls. Perks of a spinal cord injury.

Martin was slightly shocked on his return to find I was missing from my room. I think he was even more shocked to find me whizzing around in my little rock world, haring up and down the corridor to the beat of Queen. He beamed from ear to ear. He was so proud and so was I. I was ready for my big girl pants now.

Now one of the most memorable moments that make us still roar with laughter today was about to happen. I looked at the clock in my room and felt really chuffed that I had managed two and a half hours on my second day as Karen helped me to transfer back into bed (I felt I was already getting the hang of this transfer board malarky). Someone from physio then popped in to take the board away as it belonged to their department.

Martin was chatting away, barely giving the air around us a chance to breathe. He made Karen and me both laugh when he told us of his conversation with the shop assistant in M&S.

'I'm after some large Bridget Jones-style knickers,' he had said.

'I'm sorry, sir, we don't do them in your size.' Karen and I were in stitches. The three of us were chatting and having a laugh, with me back in the comfort of my bed, content from the great progress I had made. Karen seemed more interested in hanging out for a chat with us than going to get on with her other chores. I asked her about the slide board, and who would be bringing one to me tomorrow since mine had just been taken away?

'Oh, once you've been signed off, Nikki, you get to make your own.'

'Huh?'

'Oh yes, as soon as we get you into the woodwork class you get to make your own.' Her face looked scarily normal, with no hint of a smile. Martin started sniggering and I laughed too, albeit a little nervously.

'No, I'm deadly serious. You get to sand it, put a bit of your own design on and then it's yours to keep.'

Martin was gone, tears rolling down his face…

'Nikki do woodwork? She hasn't got a DIY bone in her body!'

Oh, of course not, flipping Margo was at the brunt of his jokes again! I frowned at him, trying not to laugh.

'I can just see you with your pencil behind your ear…' He was hysterical now.

'Seriously, Karen, are you kidding me here? Do I *really* have to go to woodwork?' I wasn't able to fully absorb this. I felt like I was in a scene from Candid Camera.

'Everyone does, love… you'll see,' she said as she skipped off out of the room, her ponytail bobbing on the back of her head. She brought another nurse back to confirm what she had just told me. Martin just looked at my face and another giggling fit ensued. Great, things were getting better and better!

When he was getting ready to go home later that afternoon, Martin was still smirking about my upcoming woodwork lesson. He kissed me on the forehead.

'Bye, Chippendale.' I pulled him in for a hug, taking in the smell of his aftershave.

I was starting to feel the effects of the day, aching and overwhelmed with exhaustion. He told me how proud he was of me and that he would be back four days later on his day off. It was quite a wrench saying goodbye; every inch of me wanted to be returning home with him to snuggle up in our comfy bed with our dogs asleep beside us. I begged him to FaceTime me with the doggies over the next few days. Then he was gone.

Needing to distract myself from feeling so alone suddenly, I chose to focus on some goals. I grabbed a new notebook from my bedside table, feeling liberated at being able to reach things for myself now. What could I aim for before Martin came back? I was pretty sure I would be signed off to do wheelchair transfers by the time he came back on Thursday, but what else could I push to be signed off for? I recalled OT saying one of the next stages was a transfer onto a toilet, now that was a must! Perhaps then they would pull this damn tube out of my pee hole, *that* would my biggest wish right now; the constant fear of a threatening bladder spasm was freaking me out. They seemed to be getting more intense and in turn causing me more distress. I also set myself a goal to endure being in my wheelchair for three hours by the time he returned. Judging by the banding pain just starting to set in, it was going to be tough— maybe two was more realistic. I couldn't wait to set my physio goals and was itching for my first session so I could get started with this. It seemed that learning to withstand being in a wheelchair was its own form of physio for now though.

I checked my phone; Martin was already dining out on the woodwork joke. He had posted on Facebook before he'd even left the hospital car park with a picture of a woman in a white hard hat and protective safety glasses, flashing her extendable tape measure; he took great pleasure in telling the world how amused he was by my forthcoming woodwork class.

'Well, just you wait,' I thought. 'I'll show you!'

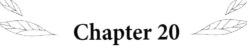

Chapter 20

Head Out of the Sand

The next four days flew by. There was so much to learn and take in. It would take about two hours to get washed and dressed in the morning, with the mini marathon using up a great deal of my energy. After my wash, (which I got no assistance with), I was now able to shuffle and lift my bum just enough to wriggle and pull up my own pants and leggings. It took about twenty minutes to get each leg in and pull the leggings on. I was able to get my bra on too; after much writhing around I would fumble with the clasp and twist it back before looping my arms through. However, getting my socks on seemed to be a tall order, a step too far. I would press my buzzer when I got to this stage and ask for a nurse to assist me. Who knew that getting dressed could be such a tribulation for a person? Something else I would never take for granted in the future, I thought.

I had to push through extreme feelings of exhaustion. I lay there almost in tears having just got dressed and considered remaining in bed; well, others on the ward seemed to! It took every ounce of willpower but, somehow, I managed to push through; I knew I had to keep moving forwards. I managed to slide myself across to the wheelchair just as Flo arrived from OT. She bounced in with her beaming smile and contagious laughter. Miss Positivity. God, I needed it. I was surprised to hear that Flo felt I was ready to move on to the next transfer stage, albeit I had only been here for a few days.

'Our woodwork teacher is on holiday this week, Nikki. I've decided you seem like someone who wouldn't want to wait, so I thought we would just progress to the next stage.' She obviously had me sussed! She showed me a process known as "lift and shift", whereby you use your arms to bridge you from the bed to the wheelchair, and lift your bum and shift your weight across to plop yourself down, job done, no transfer board required.

We practised it a couple of times and I passed the test with flying colours. The lift and shift was to become my new passport to getting in and out of bed, and a lot more to come. The slide board had been made redundant already, and to think that I had been racking my brain for a personal design to put on it during woodwork! I had even practised drawing a little moon and stars logo in my notebook, around which I was going to write my favourite quote before varnishing it. Cheesy I know, but if I was going to have to make the damn thing and take it home as a reminder, I might as well write something meaningful... no longer required though. Yet again it seemed that by fully accepting something, a little bit of magic had happened. I would save this piece of news to tell Martin face-to-face, I decided; let him relish in his picture of me with planes, saws and files at my workbench for now.

Flo took me for a visit to the OT department. She accompanied me downstairs, letting me do most of the wheeling. Even this early on I sensed the respectful distance being given to allow my independence; or maybe it was a ploy to make us learn faster. We got in the lift and, as I swivelled myself around and reached up for the button, I was confronted with a view of myself from every angle. There was a full mirror on the back wall and polished metal on both sides and the lift doors. I diverted my eyes everywhere I could to avoid seeing the reflection; I didn't want to see myself in a wheelchair... not yet.

Flo showed me around the OT department which was huge. A large "play" area in the corner reminded me of dropping my girls off at nursery school with its tables on which were an array of puzzles and games to aid dexterity. The kitchen was split in half; one end with adapted units and lowered work surfaces for permanent wheelchair users and the other end a full-sized kitchen area. I would claim that as my workspace. The rest of the OT department was a mock-up home, with a bathroom and bedroom to practise transfer skills and getting dressed.

I was just weighing up what areas I thought were going to be beneficial for me when a dreaded bladder spasm caught me off guard. I froze, struggling to breathe and trying to restrain my groan. Close to tears, I asked Flo to take me back to the ward. This time it had been worse than ever. There was an impending feeling of a full-blown panic attack that seemed to be brought on by being so far away from the ward. I needed some reassurance from a nurse and felt I would be safer back there. Surely this couldn't be normal?

Flo took control of the wheelchair and briskly wheeled me back to the ward. I was a whimpering mess when the ward sister came and spoke to me. I was instantly struck by her kindness, reassured by her stroking my hair as we talked about my spasms and how they overwhelmed me. She seemed at a loss to understand why I was getting them but reassured me that once I'd learnt how to do a transfer to a toilet, they would look at getting the catheter removed and perhaps *that* would sort the problem out. I couldn't wait. My lady minions would have a chance to prove their worth.

My psychosis seemed like a distant memory by now, something I had left far behind in the A&E department at the N&N. However, the mental health team had told me to expect some sort of psychiatric assessment whilst at Sheffield. They had indicated that it would be similar to the non-intrusive care I had received from them during my stay. Oh, how wrong they were. I was visited by two psychiatrists the next day who were to invade the inner workings of my mind in a way that was cold and clinical and very intrusive.

Two young men (is it just me getting older or do these professionals nowadays look *far* too young?) swept into my room where I was sitting in my wheelchair. It took me by surprise. They both looked very formal in their sombre suits and ties, more like private investigators than doctors of psychiatry.

'Hello, Nicola, we are here from the psychiatric team, is it convenient to talk to you?'

I instantly felt uncomfortable when they told me that this meeting would take over an hour, with the possibility of a further appointment if everything wasn't covered that day. It sounded like more of an interrogation than a friendly chat.

I wheeled myself behind "Sherlock and Dr Watson" and followed them into a private room for our confidential conversation. I felt the need to explain about my spasms just in case one occurred during our talk, so as not to surprise them if I were to randomly start deep breathing and groaning. They said it was fine, although I sensed a slight feeling of discomfort as if I'd just told them I'd got my period or something! I wondered how many mental health patients they had dealt with that had just broken their back and were in a wheelchair.

The Spanish Inquisition started. Despite my explaining my discomfort at merely sitting in my wheelchair and how I wasn't yet adjusted to it, they tirelessly interrogated me about my childhood and every member of my family; achingly dragging through my entire life from my first childhood memory, up to the current day, retracing occurrences of any mental health problems such as depression along the way. Now I am a "wear my heart on my sleeve" kind of girl, so I told them everything, getting lost at times as I weaved my way through as many memories as I could. One of them had the job of scribbling shorthand notes of my every word, whilst the other (possibly more senior) psychiatrist played the role of chief interrogator. Both of them were expressionless with a lukewarm demeanour which made me feel like I was disclosing my life to a stone wall. It was the most draining hour of my life, which on checking my watch was nearer one and a half hours. My stomach sank when I was asked if I would mind meeting again since they hadn't quite covered everything. What? I agreed, knowing full well I would try and find a way to escape another meeting with these two cold fish.

I left the room and wheeled back to my bed where I immediately had a spasm, making me cry out for a nurse who rushed in to assist me. As she released the valve on my catheter, we discovered I had wet myself. I had bypassed it again. My tears flowed as I got myself back into bed. The spasm was the final straw. It felt a like dark heavy chasm had been opened up inside me; I felt overwhelmed and mentally drained.

I rang Martin, who was furious that I had been put through the whole ordeal. Here I was, adapting to my new surroundings and by all accounts doing really well, enduring the wheelchair and suchlike, then these strangers had come in and started scraping out the insides of my head, which seemed not only unnecessary but also cruel, he said.

'Don't speak to them again, not without me being there.' I felt comforted by his love and protection and also reassured that he would be with me if I had to face the mind police again.

Later that day, I wheeled myself down to the physio room for a talk with a charity called Back Up. I braved the journey down in the lift by myself, something I'm not keen on at the best of times, let alone in a wheelchair. I was filled with panic, worried that not only I might get my wheels caught in the doors or that the lift could break down with me in it, but also that I could have a bladder spasm at any moment, giving some poor unsuspecting stranger a scare.

Thankfully I made it, feeling chuffed with myself as I wheeled into the physio room, looking just as confident as the others who had already gathered. There were about eight of us and as I reversed into a space amongst the other wheelchairs it was apparent that some people had been in the unit for quite some time, and were seemingly comrades. One chap had been here for ten long months and I found myself intrigued to find out more but was too timid to ask. I wanted to know everything about these people; they all had spinal injuries like me and were more at home with things. I could see some had difficulty moving their heads as if they had a stiff neck caused by sleeping awkwardly. Others had arms that twitched or stiffened, affected by spasticity, or hands that were unable to clasp or grip things. I wanted to learn as much as I could and as quickly as possible.

Well, Back Up couldn't have done the job better. These three really cool guys came to give us the presentation. One was a tetraplegic who came in driving his motorised chair with a tube which he kept sucking on (I ignorantly thought he was thirsty, but now realise it was a ventilator). The second was a paraplegic with a complete injury, seated in a manual wheelchair which looked far less cumbersome than mine. The third chap, who was giving the talk, was an "incomplete" injury like myself, also in a wheelchair. He explained the details of his accident, how he had hit a large stone and been thrown from his racing bike coming down a mountain. A fleeting thought crossed my mind; I prayed we wouldn't go around the room *all* sharing the nature of our accidents in a group therapy kind of way. Luckily, we didn't.

The presentation on SCIs was given in such a clear and accessible way that even I could understand. I began to loosen up as I heard all about the spinal cord and subsequent disability; this chap really struck a chord with me. I bravely acknowledged that it *was* the whole central nervous system thing that I had not dared to imagine. The spinal cord was attached to my brain stem (this was news to me), and the signals from my brain went down my spinal cord triggering all of my body's responses from maintaining my temperature to wriggling my little toes. I imagined this thick cord of nerves like a telephone cable running down from my neck to my tailbone, encased by my vertebrae and other bony structures in the same way the skull protects our brain. The nerves can't rebuild or regenerate I learnt, which meant that a full recovery was impossible. Some messages could learn to re-route with incomplete injuries, similar to a phone line being diverted, but that would take time.

My smashed vertebrae had only dented, or nicked, my spinal cord, limiting the amount of damage to the billions of nerves, which was why I had some sensation returning. The enormity of my injury was starting to sink in. There was breaking your back and then there was spinal cord damage, both capable of happening independently of each other.

We watched a video showing three or four real life examples of SCI survivors demonstrating the level of their injury and how they had adapted to a new life with their disability. This was shown in a non-discriminatory way for all levels: first with a tetraplegic disability and a man who had learnt to use a computer with voice-activated technology. Then a paraplegic who didn't let his paralysis deter him and, with the support of Back Up, was now mountain climbing (yes, in a wheelchair) and even skiing in an adapted skidoo. Next, was an example of a chap who was half wheelchair user and half able to walk with aids. Then, last but not least, was a young woman who was walking with the use of sticks and no wheelchair. It surprised me that her level still encountered various problems such as neural pain, (which I did not like the sound of), bowel and bladder problems (equally worrying), plus the guilt of being able to walk again. More guilt… didn't I already have enough of that being a mother?

I discreetly wiped the tear trickling down my face as the programme ended and realised that I felt intrinsically connected with these people, like I was part of their team. The truth was that I had indeed become part of a family; whilst we all had different stories to tell and different levels of injury, we were *all* brave and *all* strong, united by a clearly defined lifechanging moment after which life would never be the same again.

I willingly gave all my details to Back Up to make contact with me when I got home. They would provide ongoing support as well as a whole host of activities and even adventure weekends away. When I got back to my room, I phoned Martin, without an ounce of consideration for him cooking. My words gushed down the phoneline, waxing lyrical about Back Up,

'And there's even support for partners too! I left my details with them so that they can ring me once I get home and they'll pair me up with someone who has a similar level injury to me for support…' My discovery bore the excitement of some great Eureka moment.

Martin was smiling down the other end of the phone, unbelievably proud, knowing I would start to embrace my injury from this point. He had secretly been having some concerns that I was blocking out the full reality of what a spinal cord injury meant and was relieved that I was now facing up to it. Yes, my head was well and truly out of the sand; I was a spinal cord injury survivor.

Chapter 21

A Familiar Face

The next morning and six days into my stay at Sheffield, I heard one of the nurses at the reception desk mention that a Shirley Dixon was arriving that day. I couldn't believe my ears; she was still coming here. I had beaten her to it! Well, they had better not bloody well put her in the spare bed next to me; having the curtain issue again would just finish me off! I made sure to let Connor know I didn't want to share with her and explained why.

On a brighter note, my first physio session went well, and I loved Lisa, who was my new therapist, a cheery bubbly girl with a great character and a strong Brummie accent. She made it clear she was going to push me hard and wanted to set goals. My kind of girl. She put me through my paces from our very first session, making me lift myself to a standing position from my wheelchair to hold on to the long-awaited white parallel bars. I hadn't expected to do this in my first session and was filled with pride at how I was now able to stand by myself. Walking would be the next step, but not today.

At the end of the forty-five minute session, Lisa asked me what my goals were before leaving Sheffield. I told her I wanted to be walking, and that I was aiming for the end of September, just three weeks away from now. Her expression gave nothing away; her poker face was far better than mine. We talked about setting additional goals that I hadn't even thought of, such as learning to climb stairs— obviously quite useful since we don't live in a bungalow! My first goal was to be able to stand and walk with a Zimmer frame (unassisted) and to do a 180-degree turn with the frame which Lisa demonstrated to me. She set the target for ten days, which seemed fairly easy to me. She recommended that I take part in the extra sessions such as core classes where we would lie on the large double-sized exercise beds to work on our abs, glutes and quads, all of which needed building up again, all playing a vital role in being able to walk. Funny how we never think how many muscles are involved in the thing we take for granted every day of our lives.

As soon as I got back to my room, I grabbed my notebook and wrote down my new goal— to do a 180-degree turn with the Zimmer frame; but I decreased the time down to *seven* days. If I could knock three days off Lisa's goal, it was bound to move things on quicker, right? I wheeled over to my timetable and circled the core strengthening class at lunchtime the next day; I would go to *everything*.

I found it strange and a little lonely that I seemed to be the only one wheeling around the ward as I went for a little "stroll" in my chair, so decided to go and make friends. Firstly, I wheeled into Danny's room.

I wheeled up to Danny's bed and he seemed pleased to

see me. I asked why he was still in bed, and he explained that he always had to wait to be hoisted into his chair and some days he just wasn't up to it. It was apparent he had a much worse injury with far more to deal with than me. Two broken arms made it difficult for him to have the strength to wheel himself, plus he was paralysed from the chest down and needing full assistance with everything. It stirred incredible compassion in me; I was haunted with the realisation that it could so easily have been me in his place.

I discovered Danny had a little boy aged just two, whom he hadn't seen in the last few months since his accident, mainly due to a breakup with his boy's mother. He missed him terribly and was counting the days until his in-laws brought him in for a visit. It stirred up the memory of how I used to miss Chloe when she had moved county to try living with her dad, how powerless I felt as a parent and the depth of yearning for my child whom I wanted to hold and protect with my entire being.

After chatting to Danny, I wheeled off to check out some other rooms on the ward.

Across from my room on the opposite side of the nurse's station was the largest room, with six hospital beds, similar to my room at the N&N. I noticed a burly young guy sitting in his wheelchair chatting to a lady in the bed nearest the glass partition and I heard him say her name. It was Shirley!

Thank God they had put her in a different room to me.

I decided to wheel up to her and say hello. Why not? Part of me wanted her to know I had got here before her, which isn't kind of me, I know. Another part selfishly wanted the familiarity of someone from my home ground of Norfolk. I waited at the end of her bed awkwardly, while this chap who was obviously from an SCI charity finished his conversation. She seemed to know I was there but didn't glance down at me from her bed.

Finally, he left.

'Hello, Shirley.'

She looked confused.

'Hello, do I know you?' Of course, she had never caught a glimpse of me in the N&N; she had no idea who I was.

'It's Nikki, I was next to you at the N&N.' The penny dropped.

'Oh, Nikki… how come you're here already?' A shocked, confused look came over her face. I immediately felt slightly guilty and abandoned my smugness. She was on flat bed rest waiting for her assessments before they allowed her full upright privileges and I could see she seemed confused and upset by this. She was obviously a bit older than me, I guessed in her sixties or possibly seventies, with shortish auburn-brown hair and a pale complexion. She seemed a little apprehensive which spurred me into overdrive, chatting and gesticulating fervently, explaining what I'd learnt so far and telling her how kind everyone was, that she would get a bed shower and how it was uncomfortable being put in a wheelchair at first. At this point she interrupted me.

'Oh, they put me in a wheelchair at Cambridge, so I'm familiar with that.'

The competitive streak re-ignited and on hearing this I found myself hoping she hadn't walked with the parallel bars yet. We chatted a little longer, making polite conversation until I decided to leave.

'I'll see you around when you're up and wheeling.' I had done the neighbourly thing; I'd gone to find her and introduce myself. Hopefully, we would tolerate each other during our stay here.

I had my first ward visit the next day, which is where a team of specialists come to visit you in your room. This included the spinal consultant, the ward sister, a discharge nurse, a physio assistant and various others. I found it quite intimidating being down at waist height in the chair, unable to take in all their names, knowing full well I wouldn't remember a single one of them. I was feeling insignificant and rather inferior. Was it my imagination or were they speaking slowly and loudly to me, as if I was a bit deaf?

My consultant was warm and friendly. He went through my notes explaining my injury in great detail, more for the benefit of his team than myself I think, telling us all about my mobility progress and details of my spinal "fusion". They asked me some questions and I think I caused quite a stir when we talked about bowels, especially when my consultant asked if I could pass wind.

I didn't understand his Asian accent, so he said it again, more clearly. 'Are you able to fart, Nicola?'

'Oh yes, erm... absolutely. And please call me Nikki.'

'And are you able to hold on to a fart?'

I looked up, confused

'Why would I want to do that?' I asked, innocently.

A few of the staff tittered and I realised how funny my response had been. The consultant just smiled. It would be a sign that I had good sphincter muscle control; well, I would try it next time, I decided.

My consultant said that I didn't need bowel care anymore after I described all the ins and outs of my bowel movements to him. He even looked a bit surprised, concerned maybe, when I said that I had managed to pass a couple of movements on my own, without the bowel care. Maybe I hadn't needed it for a while? Who knows? All that mattered was I wouldn't need it from this point on. Just a laxative was required in the evening and no more nurses poking me up my rear end. Hallelujah! It was time to say goodbye to bowel care at long last. My minion men had done their job! They would soon be able to party, hopefully with their wives.

Chapter 22

Landing in the Stars

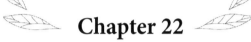

Martin arrived, larger than life, a full five days since I last saw him. Well, I say larger than life… but I wasn't the only one losing weight around here; it would seem that the torture of standing at a hot griddle in a blistering hot and cramped kitchen was affecting his portliness. I had started to notice towards the end of N&N that every time he came bounding in, he either had a new shirt, new jacket or shoes on! The one consistent thing was his beaming smile, always pleased, relieved to see me. He was laden with gifts including my long-awaited MacBook Air.

'How was the woodwork lesson, darling?'

I smugly told him how I had dodged the need for a slide board. No woodwork class required. I proudly told him how I had been signed off to do lift and shift to my wheelchair and even on and off the toilet now too. He looked somewhat relieved to hear this progress, having probably given far more credence to the prognosis of being incontinent than I had.

Whilst back on toilet talk, I was now proudly able to do my number twos on the toilet! Meaning no more demoralising clean-ups. The only problem at the moment though, was that the excruciating bladder spasms followed immediately after vacating my bowels, causing me to pull the emergency cord for all the nurses to come running. They would find me hanging on to the sidebars for dear life, trying to breathe my way through the contraction. If anything could have made me give up my battle and indulge in some full-blown self-pity, these spasms could. But giving up wasn't an option, not if I wanted to get home to my doggies before they forgot me or get back to the loving arms of Martin. I kept reminding myself that the spasms were not permanent, nothing ever is; I just needed to push through them, one at a time. It would soon pass.

Martin and I spent our time wheeling around the ward, with me proudly showing him my new home. I took him down in the lift and he laughed as I spun 180 degrees, landing in perfect alignment to press the button. I squinted briefly at my reflection. My hair had grown long, and I had a few extra grey highlights, but I liked my new skinny arms and my face looked so much better with less chubbiness.

'Didn't think it would take you long to get the hang of that thing, Stirling Moss,' he said, looking the wheelchair up and down. I felt smug. Look at how far I'd come since my first day here. It was hard to believe it was only a week ago.

On the ground floor, I showed him the physio and OT departments and we peered through some closed doors at the hydra pool which I was looking forward to using at some point. We discovered a full-size sports hall, like the kind you had at school. There was a wheelchair basketball session taking place, with people who were obviously from an outside club as they seemed too professional to be patients.

'You should give that a go, you'd enjoy it,' Martin suggested.

I cringed at the thought. Apart from the fact that I couldn't really see myself participating in wheelchair activities, I couldn't bear the thought of moving around too much in this damn chair since the tube from my catheter would rub against my lady bits if I moved and would invariably trigger a spasm, so I kept myself as still as I could. They were happening nearly every hour now, and they weren't getting any easier to handle.

We sat having a coffee together in the library, where we laughed at the oversized goldfish who kept head-banging the bottom of their tank. Engaging in one of our *Johnny Morris* style conversations, we laughed, with me tailoring my laughter to not trigger a spasm. After our coffee, Martin accompanied me to physio. I felt like a child being delivered to school and like the sad parent that wanted to stay and help, Martin was disappointed when Lisa said he couldn't stay to watch. She promised him that should there be any earth-shattering moments we would call him on his mobile. This was to respect the privacy of other patients, even though there were only two others in the gym at the time.

Having only done bench exercises in my previous session, I was happy that Lisa took me straight over to the white bars to practise standing again. After trying some lunges and testing out my balance by trying to lift one leg at a time, I begged her to let me try walking. She had to change the height of the white bars and then demonstrated how to walk about three metres using the bars for balance, turning at the end, and then returning back to the safety of the waiting chair.

Wow… As I started, I was shocked by how much more strength I had since my first attempt at walking with the frame at N&N. My legs were taking all the weight and whilst they felt a bit shaky it was easier than I had thought it would be. I reached the end after about ten steps and managed to do the turn slowly and steadily. I was beaming. So was Lisa. My co-ordination was even better on my return to the wheelchair; my hands alternating as they reached for the cold white bar, my eyes focused on the wall ahead, my legs taking baby steps from left to right foot.

I begged her to let me call Martin to come back and watch; this was that earth-shattering moment. I wanted him to see this, they had been wrong; I was going to walk! I was midway along the bars for the second time when I noticed him standing there in the middle of the gym, tears rolling down his face, overwhelmed with emotion. Honest to God, it was like something out of a movie. The cliché happy ending. He was crying, I was crying, Lisa had even welled up. I don't think I've ever been so overwhelmed other than when holding my daughters for the first time.

I tried to stay focused; I didn't want to wobble and end this badly. Lisa asked me to give some more hip action to the movement and I tried my best to make it more natural and look a little less like a Thunderbirds puppet. I reached my chair and sat down, beaming from ear to ear, zapped of all energy, but so satisfied.

Martin had been videoing me, which of course was going to be splashed all over Facebook. Annoyingly I had one of my pink and black gloves Velcroed to my bum which looked a bit like a cow's udder hanging off my arse! Why hadn't anyone told me? Hopefully, people wouldn't notice.

The remaining lesson was spent balancing on wobble boards and practising other balance exercises. Martin stayed and watched as the physio room was now empty. It appeared I had some balance on the right leg and but little to nothing on the left leg. I was like one of those Fisher-Price Weebles from the seventies— "Weebles wobble but they don't fall down".

I felt on cloud nine after my physio session; there was only one thing now standing in my way… *Cathy*! The damn catheter and its incessant bladder spasms. I had googled and googled but felt defeated in my search for a cause. The ward sister had decided to put me on another course of antibiotics in case it was a urine infection (déjà vu), but I knew it wasn't.

I mentioned to Martin in the lift what a relief it was to not have had a spasm during the physio lesson and must have talked it up because just as we got back to the ward, I had another one and Martin had to help me breathe through it. I called out to Karen who was outside my room by the food trolley to come and help me and check I hadn't wet myself. I hadn't. I was beside myself with worry that I had something severely wrong with me since every other patient on the ward had a catheter strapped to their leg like me, and yet I was the only one having these damn spasms.

Martin left the following day for his arduous journey back to Norfolk with a list of instructions for his next visit the following weekend. If my ward meeting went as planned this week, he would hopefully be taking me for a day trip to the Tropic Glammies in Birmingham. That was if my catheter situation was improved; there was no way I could go with the current state of play. I felt confident it would be sorted by then though and had butterflies in my tummy thinking about my "day release".

With Martin gone, I decided to lie on my bed for a little rest. I was mid lift and shift when I was struck with another spasm. I froze, shouting out for a nurse to help me. The ward sister came running to help me. I had wet myself again.

'Right, it's time that catheter came out,' she declared. Just like that. She decided that it could possibly be my body's way of telling me to get rid of Cathy, and seeing as I was already on antibiotics, we should take it out now and see what happened.

Now apparently only a lucky few with an SCI get use of their bladder back. It was touch and go whether or not my brain signals would get through to co-ordinate and release the urethral sphincter muscle when the bladder was full. Failing to do so would mean I would need to use little mini catheters (a bit like carton drink straws) and learn to insert them myself. This filled me with horror. The discomfort going on around my tinkle tunnel would *not* be conducive to me trying to stick a Kia-Ora straw up it!

The nurse came and I yelped as the catheter was swiftly and painfully removed. It was out. I was free at last. I lay there in disbelief. For the first time in nine weeks, I had nothing attached to me. Cathy was gone. All I had to do now was pray that my lady minions would do their job and get it all working again for me.

Now it's an automatic process going for a wee. Your brain receives a message when your bladder is full and off you trot to the toilet. But because I had had a catheter in for so long, my brain seemed to have forgotten what the sensations felt like and it was hard to tell whether my bladder was full or not.

Half an hour later I suspected it may be time as there was a tenderness in my lower abdomen when I pressed it, so I transferred into my wheelchair as quickly as I could to set off for the toilet which was at the far end of the corridor past Shirley's ward. Connor stopped me for a quick chat at the nurse's station, but I soon told him I had to go and wheeled quickly to the toilet. Yes, it was more definite to me now.

I flipped the arm up on my wheelchair at the same time as expertly reversing in next to the toilet. I quickly flipped the foot pedals out of the way at the same time as fixing the brake on and just as I started the lift and shift… my muscles decided they couldn't hold a second longer. I was trying to get my leggings down and sit myself on the toilet as it uncontrollably gushed down my legs. God, it felt good. A long blissful wee. I didn't care. The tube was out, and I knew I could get there quicker next time.

I pulled the cord for assistance. Connor came to my rescue

'Well, I nearly made it,' I laughed with my leggings around my ankles and a puddle of wee at my feet. Connor went off to my room to get me some fresh clothes and when he returned, he chucked some fresh leggings and pants at me.

'You know where the laundry room is!' he said smirking, and left. Oh, right okay, don't help me then. Tough love!

It took me a good twenty minutes or so to get sorted, leaving the puddle for someone else to clear up, and then I wheeled myself down to the laundry room where I experienced further dilemmas of being a wheelchair user; getting into the right position to open the washing machine door, leaning down to pick up the powder, angling it just right to get my washing in and switch it all on. God, I was shattered. Life was incredibly tiring in a wheelchair.

That night I was given a commode. It was planted next to my bed as I lay there talking to my lady minions. They didn't let me down. I was up and down doing the lift and shift all through the night, and when the nurse came to scan my bladder to check it was fully emptying it turned out it was. Result! My minions had done their job! Their husbands were waiting for them and it was party time!

The next day at physio, yet another breakthrough took place. Lisa brought out the Zimmer frame for me to start practising with (I still had five days to reach our goal). Memories came back of that last day in August when I'd used the Zimmer frame at the N&N. This time there were no white knuckles though, my legs were taking all the weight, with no nurses supporting me on either side. It took a little practise to get the hang of it, but I was soon able to take seven or eight steps. I asked if Lisa would teach me how to turn around. I watched her demonstration and instantly knew I wanted to try it. Lisa smiled at me and agreed to let me have a go; she was a pushover!

I managed it perfectly, a bit like a three-point turn, and sat back down on the exercise bench. Lisa asked me to do it again.

'Well, you smashed that goal,' she laughed. I had, and five days early too; the morning exercises and extra classes I had been coming to were showing their results.

Now, I know I sound like a boastful child, but please allow me to indulge in one more of my favourite highlights.

My ward round the following day was to take place in one of the meeting rooms instead of in my room. Lisa came to meet me outside five minutes beforehand with the Zimmer frame for me to have a little practise on. I was going to walk into the meeting! She would be right behind me with my wheelchair.

A few minutes later the door opened, and I was called in. I focused carefully on each step as I shuffled in with the frame to a room full of clinicians and nurses. My spinal consultant was overjoyed, and everyone applauded me as I sat down in my wheelchair. I would have curtsied if I could!

We talked about the Glammies, and I was given full permission to go and have a good time and even indulge in a glass of prosecco if I wanted. I would need to practise a car transfer with physio and then, with Martin as my companion and co-pilot of my wheelchair, we would be off… day release! I was so excited.

Towards the end of the conversation, I asked my consultant when I would hear any news on a discharge date. I know I had only been there twelve days, but it felt like a lot longer.

'Well, Nikki, based on your recovery so far, and depending on whether you can keep up the level of hard work you are demonstrating right now, we have given you a provisional discharge date of the fourth of October.' Did I hear that right? My face showed complete disbelief. I asked him to tell me again just to make certain I hadn't heard it wrong. I hadn't. They were going to release me on 4 October. Just *four* days after the end of September which had been my goal.

"Aim for the moon, if you miss you still land in the stars."
I had truly landed in the stars again.

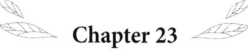

Chapter 23

Making Friends with the Enemy

With Cathy gone, my mood and my enthusiasm shot up to new heights. I was free, able to wriggle and move about to my heart's content with no impending fear of triggering a bladder spasm. I could even stand up from my wheelchair a little, so long as the brake was firmly put on and it was right behind me. I loved being able to stand and put my clothes back on the rail in my wardrobe, it felt so liberating. I wonder if a toddler feels the same excitement when they first find their legs and can stand up by themselves?

I had been moved to one of the private ensuite rooms that I had had my eye on. I loved it. It was reminiscent of a double room in a Travel Lodge or some other budget hotel. A little more basic maybe, and a tad clinical with its obligatory surgical waste bin at the end of my bed. But there was a funky little bedside table with a drawer, and an Argos-style single wardrobe. The ensuite was bright and roomy and was also a wet room. I was loving the independence of being able to shower myself now: this was done by holding a shower head over myself whilst safely sitting on the toilet and then doing a lift and shift into my wheelchair with just a towel across me and wheeling myself back to my bed to get dressed.

It felt like I was starting to come back to the land of the living. I had made my own little mock dressing table by the window with a redundant over-bed table which I'd claimed from my previous room. It had my mirror, brush and a few makeup bits neatly organised on it and I would sit in my wheelchair in front of the mirror and blow dry my long hair, which was a physio exercise in itself; I was surprised at just how many core muscles are required to hold a hairdryer above your head. I would even put on some Tropic makeup with a smidge of lip gloss when my hair was done. God, it made me feel so good; Nikki Rodwell was back.

There were between ten to fifteen patients on Osborne 1, and I would wheel around the ward in the hope of finding someone to chat with. Most patients had daily visitors which made me feel a little like Billy-no-mates since I was so far away from home. The other person who, like me, was a fair way from home was Shirley.

I whizzed into Shirley's room since, like me, she was often up and about first thing in the morning. I found her sitting in her wheelchair by her bed doing some needlework, so invited her for a spin. Now on a scale of a Reliant Robin to Lamborghini for speed, Shirley was a Morris Minor in wheeling herself in a wheelchair. She didn't seem to be getting around much for practise, so I invited her to come up onto the patio with me for some fresh air. She had a nurse push her up the ramp whilst I managed to propel myself up the ramp with no assistance.

We sat and had a chat, our first proper chance to get to know each other and talk about our experiences. Poor

Shirley had been wrongly diagnosed with having a stroke initially. She had woken up in bed with a pain in her neck which turned out to be a bleed on her spinal cord. How scary is that? She was in her early seventies so a bit older than I had initially thought and was a widow. Her sons played a big part in her life; I had seen them often visit her in the N&N as did her large circle of friends, so she wasn't short of company. She told me how going to the rehab clinic in Cambridge had complicated things, that she had to re-register with her doctors before she could get support and homecare put in place. I realised at that moment how scary it must be to go home with this injury on your own, be it in a wheelchair *or* walking. I would have Martin there for me and that made the world of difference. Poor Shirley had no one. I felt great sympathy for her.

Shirley and I started meeting up daily from that point on. We would wheel to the café together or go down to physio, keeping each other company; sometimes I would wheel behind her with my legs stuck outright to push her from behind. She would laugh and apologise for being so slow. The truth was she had weakness in her arms, and it wasn't easy for her to push herself. I found myself warming to this lady who I had almost thought of as my enemy whilst in the N&N.

I invited her back to my room to see the bits I had ordered for the upcoming Glammies event. It took careful consideration to think of what would be best to wear in a wheelchair. The theme was "Carnival of Colour" and I opted for some bright psychedelic leggings for comfort and had a couple of different brightly coloured tops to choose from. I planned to dress this up with some snazzy gold trainers and some bling jewellery.

The Glammies is an event where anything goes. A few thousand ambassadors turn up from all around the UK in an array of glamourous outfits ranging from the all-out glamour queens to the sublimely ridiculous exhibitionists of all shapes and sizes. A people watcher's paradise. The first time I went four years ago, I had felt like I'd arrived at a red-carpet BAFTA affair, my mouth wide open at the dazzling surroundings and glamourous women. It was the first time I would be going with Martin and I just knew he was going to have a great time.

'Well, I have to say I think you're extremely brave going all the way to Birmingham for the day; I don't think I would do it,' Shirley said.

'Well, I'll take a spare pair of leggings just in case my bladder lets me down, but it'll be fine,' I said.

So, it's true to say that as we shared our thoughts and aimed for our shared goal of getting back to our lives in Norfolk, Shirley and I became friends. That's not to say I didn't keep up my competitive streak!

Something that played on my mind was how I had a time limit with my recovery. The maximum improvement would be made in the first six months and I was more than two months in. My cord was out of spinal shock now and I needed to maximise my recovery. Whilst I knew I could never make a 100% recovery, signals *were* getting through, a bit like Google Maps when it reroutes to avoid traffic congestion. I wasn't happy to sit around and leave things to chance; I wanted to work as best I could before I ran out of time!

I would practise standing at every opportunity, such as at my sink when cleaning my teeth. So long as I kept one hand on the unit, I could do this for just long enough to wash my face and clean my teeth. I would even try and lift one leg and test my balance whilst taking off my makeup or putting my deodorant on, always with my wheelchair right behind me or with something to grab on to. I almost felt like a naughty school child constantly pushing the limits and perhaps taking risks, but luckily, I never had an accident. Nobody had given me permission to stand and turn by holding the grab rails when using the toilet instead of doing the lift and shift I'd been taught; I hadn't been "signed off" for standing at my sink or hanging things in my wardrobe. No, I had to discover and try these things for myself. I could even reach down to pick things up from the floor if I dropped them now. There was just *one* damn thing I still couldn't do and that was put my socks on!

A new phenomenon started around this time, which I still have today. Whilst it was apparent that other patients had spasms, whereby a limb would stiffen up and fling itself out unexpectedly, I, as usual, had to be different. When my leg was at a certain angle with my foot resting on the footplate of my wheelchair, it would start to jiggle up and down of its own accord, a bit like someone rhythmically tapping their leg to some music at superfast speed. This spasm I soon discovered (thanks to Google) was called a "clonus" which was in no way painful and I would find it quite entertaining, especially since I could start and stop it at will, even with both legs at once. It would soon become my new party-piece!

My first visit to the sports hall was for basketball. Yes, I know I said I wouldn't, but I was kind of getting into this now! I was feeling much more confident in the wheelchair.

I asked Shirley if she wanted to come along, but there was an art class in the dining room which was more her thing. So I went alone, down in the lift, embracing my reflection before weaving around the corridors on the ground floor until I found the sports hall.

There were about seven or eight other patients, some of whom had just come to watch, others who were from Osborne 3 and were just as good in their wheelchairs as me. I was paired up with a chap who was probably in his mid-forties, to play dodge the wheelchair. He had to try to block me from getting past him to the other end of the badminton court and across the baseline. I wheeled back and forth, doing little wheelies as I skidded around, building up a sweat. He didn't make it easy for me.

Eventually, I faked a sideways move, tricking my way past my opponent and beating him to the finish line. The winner got to stay on. I then beat two more guys, finally being challenged by the coach himself, who took great pleasure in beating me.

At the end of the session, a few of us were trying to get a ball into the basketball net, which, believe me, is a long way up from a wheelchair. It was really difficult getting the projection to throw it up at the right angle. One of the guys got it in a couple of times which proved to me it was possible. I often say to the girls in my team that one person doing a seemingly impossible task shows that it is possible for anyone. After all, it only took one man to land on the moon to show humanity that other men would be able to do the same.

I was still trying to get the damn ball in when the session ended. Determined not to be beaten I asked one of the helpers to stay and assist me; she kept throwing the ball back to me after the missed shots. Then the inevitable happened, and of course, I did it. It felt so good as the ball plopped through the net.

This sports session had made time speed up considerably; I couldn't believe two hours had passed and I was buzzing after interacting with the others. It was no wonder that I ached so much that evening. I had demanded all my muscles wake up and get back into action.

Only two weeks after arriving at Sheffield and I hardly recognised myself. I was becoming the Evil Knievel of the wheelchair world, a very different person who had sat glaring at it from her bed, initially refusing to get in it. I even found myself rushing to vehemently defend it; I had sent a message to my mum explaining how I was going to the Glammies at the weekend, and she sent a message back saying she was surprised to hear this. When I asked why, she replied,

'Well, being you're in a wheelchair. I wouldn't have thought you would want to go,'

I saw red. What if I stayed in a wheelchair permanently? Was my life never going to continue? Would I not go out again because it was "embarrassing" being in a wheelchair?

Martin thankfully calmed me down and told me not to respond. Well, I did, but not in a hostile or confrontational way.

'It's okay, Mum, there are a few Tropic ambassadors who are in wheelchairs, I won't be the only one.'

'Oh well, you know me, I wouldn't want to draw attention to myself.'

I was well aware I would be noticed, of course; all my team and friends would be amazed to see me there not realising that I was coming. I would be going on stage too, under the spotlight and in front of a few thousand women… in my wheelchair which I was planning to decorate with little coloured streamers and stickers from the OT department, so that it too, could take part in the carnival theme. Yes, I would fully draw attention to my wheelchair which, I can proudly say, had become my friend.

Chapter 24

The Glammies

The Glammies was as big and glitzy as ever. I sat in the car with Martin in our reserved disabled space watching glamourous women teetering past in their high heels towards the entrance of the NEC centre. I was trying to pick out someone I recognised, someone from my team or anybody from Norfolk, whilst we sat and reflected for a few minutes. Martin and I had not got off to a good start that morning and were just taking a few minutes out to compose ourselves and prepare for the day.

This was my first experience of being out in public in my wheelchair, and it hadn't gone to plan so far…

Half an hour into the car journey I had asked Martin if we could pull over for a toilet stop. My bladder was still unable to last for long periods whilst rebuilding its strength. I had felt ignored as Martin drove past the "services" sign and when I questioned him, he had merely snapped at me that there would be another one. I was glad I had packed a spare pair of leggings now.

The next service station had taken a good ten minutes to come across, meaning it was far more urgent now and Martin rushed to fetch the wheelchair out of the boot of the car and put it in position for me to transfer. As I started to wheel myself towards the entrance, there was no offer of assistance from him; it was far harder pushing on uneven concrete than the smooth hospital floors. Starting to feel the stress build inside me, I asked if he would mind helping me. He grabbed the back of the wheelchair, complaining that the handles were too low for him. 'Oh well, I'm sorry, that must be very difficult for you,' I thought, biting my lip.

We found the disabled toilet and after conquering the difficult task of manoeuvring my wheelchair backwards into the cubicle whilst pulling the door closed, I successfully lifted and shifted in the nick of time. Getting out was a little tricky though. The door was too stiff to easily push open so I tried with my legs but still couldn't manage it. After yanking the handle up and down noisily, hoping that Martin would see my dilemma from the other side of the door, I finally managed to push it free. I was faced with a husband who couldn't have been any less interested, more engrossed in a conversation on his mobile phone and oblivious of my difficulty in trying to get out. I wheeled up and waited for him to finish, feeling a wave of anger in the pit of my stomach.

Once the call was finished, he pushed me towards Gregg's bakery to get something to eat and the sea of people's waistlines rushing past me made me feel quite dizzy.

'Do you want to go and wait outside?' he asked as we got

to Greggs. I thought for a second that perhaps he perceived me as an inconvenience, that it would be easier to get me out of the way, so I refused and insisted I went in with him. As we waited in the queue, Martin sensed something was wrong and tried half-heartedly to ask me what it was. I didn't want to get upset and smudge all my perfectly applied makeup, so I wheeled myself outside to wait. It was then it hit me. I was in a wheelchair; my husband had lost all sensitivity and this big day was going to be disastrous. Why had I decided to come?

A big tear plopped down my face, and I quickly tried to dry it before it streaked my makeup. People were flying past me, rushing in above my head from all angles, giving me the sense that I was invisible. Vulnerable too. It wasn't nice.

Martin arrived with two sausage rolls and after I transferred back into the car, he returned my wheelchair to the boot and I sensed things were going to get uncomfortable. They did. Martin decided to take control and demand to know what was wrong. But as ridiculous as it sounds, I didn't want to smudge my makeup so didn't want to open up for fear of crying.

'I'm fine,' I said through gritted teeth, putting on a fake smile. Sensing this wouldn't end the matter and had only served to frustrate him even more, I felt it best to be honest, telling him that I didn't want to discuss it for fear of crying and spoiling my makeup. Now Martin can be overpowering at times, perhaps bulldozing my feelings, and *this* was one such time. He would not let it rest and went on and on until I burst into tears. I screamed at him to take me back to the hospital since I would have to redo all my makeup.

I completely lost control as I cried that the whole day was now ruined. Wow. This was not going well.

Thankfully we managed to talk it out, both admitting how we felt under a huge amount of pressure. Martin was nervous about his responsibility of being "my carer" for the day and he apologised for not handling me with more sensitivity. We decided to put the experience behind us, and I did my best to patch up my blotchy eyes.

So, despite a shaky start, we were here, and Martin was telling me how proud he was of just how far I had come. I had been true to my word back at the beginning of August saying that I was *not* going to miss this Glammies! This felt like my celebration in many ways, of how much I had achieved so far in my recovery.

I could feel every bump on the pavement as Martin pushed me in; every crack in the slabs of concrete gave a little jolt resonating up my spine. We were soon through the doors of the NEC with the swarms of women moving in all directions.

My frontline leader, who was one of the initial women to start Tropic, was the first friendly face that I bumped into. She had tears in her eyes as she rushed over to hug me.

'Nikki, it's so brilliant to see you, pet.' I had never been so pleased to hear that warm Lancashire tone. Tonia is a truly wonderful human being; a warm, loving and kind lady whom I greatly admire. She is a fantastic leader, with the inherent ability to make you feel like you're one of her best friends despite managing a team of thousands of women. On her visits to Norfolk, I would lose myself in her motivational talks, in awe of her wicked sense of humour and inspired by her down-to-earth stories that instantly resonated with me. She is truly one of life's gems and I was immediately reassured as she leant down to hug me, glad I had come.

As we went into the venue, more and more women came up to greet me and before long I was surrounded by my whole team. We chatted, took photos and drank prosecco with Martin always on the periphery, standing by in case I needed his help. It all felt slightly surreal, the glitz and glamour going on around me, with the buzz and excitement of everyone getting ready for the start. I usually get butterflies in my tummy at this event but today they were magnified.

I was relieved that our table, whilst not in the best position to see the stage and Lord Sugar, was right by the toilets. This suited me today, reassuring me that I would avoid any accidents. The colossal venue easily housed the three thousand excited women buzzing around finding their seats. There were oversized screens strategically placed to show those of us further back what was happening on stage. The stage was at the centre of the audience with a large circular standing area which revolved, then there were two long catwalks extending either side from it leading to exit ramps. It was all quite magnificent.

The show began and I was overwhelmed with emotion, looking around the surrounding tables which were full of the girls from my team.

First up for recognition from my team were two beautiful ladies who had been promoted to manager. I wheeled myself through the crowds to the edge of the stage where I put on my brake and stood up, holding on to the edge of the stage to make sure they could see me as I clapped and whooped for them. They saw me as they descended the stage down the ramp, cameras flashing in all directions. The atmosphere was electric.

Next up was one of my ladies who had been promoted to executive, the same leadership title as me, and her newly developing team were all here to celebrate with her. I couldn't have been prouder as I watched her receive her flowers from Susie Ma with everyone cheering and clapping as she paraded the stage.

Before I knew it, it was my turn. My team and I had reached our first £1 million milestone. I panicked that I wouldn't make it onto the stage quick enough as my manager weaved me through the crowds towards the ramp. We made it and just as my name was announced, she gave me a firm push and let go of me to wheel myself to centre stage.

Susie Ma, the founder, looked confused to see me in a wheelchair as she hugged me. I reassured her that I was fine and that it was a bit of a long story. I positioned myself on the centrepiece with the other ambassadors who had also achieved million milestones. As it revolved, I could see Martin at the edge of the stage, clapping me. I held my bottle of bubbly up in the air, beaming from ear to ear, feeling like to a celebrity. As he got his camera out to take a picture, I put my brake on and decided to stand. I love this photo today as it shows a picture of happiness and pride. I was so full of hope.

My manager rushed up the exit ramp to help wheel me

down, which was scarily out of control as she was a little tipsy and teetering in high heels. Skidding to a halt at the bottom, we realised we needed to rush back to the other side again since they were now announcing recognition for the Cambodia trip.

So, there I was again upon the brightly lit stage with 200 other ambassadors who had all won the trip as well, all of us whooping with excitement knowing we would be off to Cambodia and Vietnam. I was the only one in the group photo in a wheelchair, but in my brightly-coloured attire and with my face beaming, I look bloody fantastic.

Photographs all taken and safely back down the ramp, the rest of the day passed in a blur. I had two or three glasses of prosecco which went to my head a little and by 3.00 p.m. I was feeling exhausted. I rested my head on the table and leant forward to stretch out my back.

'Sweetheart, you've done so well— why don't we make a move?'

Martin was right. We still had a two-hour journey back to Sheffield. I wheeled around the tables and said my goodbyes, and then it was all over.

Like Cinderella after the ball, I was back in my room on the ward, over-tired and feeling slightly pathetic. I asked Karen to help get me ready for bed which she reluctantly did and after some pain meds I settled down to rest with tears trickling down my face. I felt like a schoolchild who had just returned to their boarding school after a weekend visit home. It was a strange, yearning feeling, which made me realise it was time to get out of here and get back to normal life as soon as possible. Well, as normal as normal would be now.

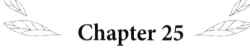

Chapter 25

Final Push

It was decided that I would remain on Osborne 1 until my discharge in ten days' time. I was happy and settled with my private room so the powers that be allowed me to bypass being moved to a bed on Osborne 3; I was still able to use the dining room though. Poor Shirley on the other hand, had been moved twice already, and I could see what an upheaval it was for her. I almost wished I could trade places to save her having this distress. I felt guilty that I was enjoying my time here, whilst she seemed to encounter one problem after another. She hadn't succeeded in getting her bladder back either, which I most definitely decided I couldn't trade places with in a million years. No friendship could go quite that far!

My positivity diary was filling up rapidly. Whilst there were challenges, and my future still seemed somewhat uncertain, I was finding happiness and purpose. I had so much to be grateful for. God forbid, I could have hit my head and not be here to tell the tale, something I hardly dare let myself think about, and then, I only had to wheel around the ward to see just how lucky I was. There were so many less fortunate than me.

One of the rooms in Osborne 3 was occupied by six high dependency patients who were motionless on their backs connected to oxygen tanks and drips. Cervical collars and head blocks held them perfectly rigid, and it brought a brief flashback of my time in A&E when I had been in the same predicament; I realised just how far I'd come since then. I observed these patients from the doorway, respecting their privacy since they all had their eyes closed, and the room had a sense of ICU about it despite the doors being open. I wondered if these were the patients that Connor had mentioned could be here for eighteen months or so, or, in fact, if they *ever* got to leave? It gave me the shivers; it was overwhelming to think that if I had hit the wall at a slightly different angle that could have been me.

Gratitude would come over me in waves and absence was definitely making my heart grow fonder as well, making me realise that I had the most wonderful husband in the entire world to go home to. He loved me as if his life depended on it and I couldn't wait to get back to the security of our love and laughter and, of course, our two beautiful dogs whom I yearned to cuddle. I wrote in my diary smaller things that became important to me too, such as how lucky I was to have the comfort of food being brought to me three times a day. Well, sometimes four, as I was starting to get snack attacks at night now which were satiated by the sneaky stash of leftover sandwiches and snacks that the night porter sometimes had on the late-night drinks trolley. I was putting a few pounds back on already.

I was asked by the sister on the ward if I would wheel myself back to my old room and introduce myself to a new lady who had just arrived on the ward and reassure her what the hospital was like from my experience. I spent nearly an hour with her and could see her tension slowly dissipate as we chatted. From this point on, I seemed to become an advocate for the ward, chosen to go and chat to people and cheer them up, which of course I loved. I would wheel myself up to the side of their bed and, so long as they didn't look asleep, I would bounce into their space with a 'Hi, I'm Nikki, it's really nice to meet you.'

If I wasn't in physio, OT, or having coffee with Shirley, I was wheeling around the ward looking for people to chat to, trying to spur them on a little. I was intrigued to hear all the extraordinary stories of how their spinal cords had been damaged, from falling off a ladder and diving accidents to slipping on a rug at home and falling down the stairs with flip flops on (I made a mental note *not* to wear flip flops in the house anymore). I would always decline to share my story though. I just couldn't find the words to say I'd fallen from a roof because I knew they would ask, 'What were you doing on a roof?'

To contain my excitement about going home, I set about drawing a countdown calendar to put on my wall so that it was the first and the last thing I saw each day. The A4 piece of paper with my primary-grade artwork would have a large cross drawn through each day, giving me butterflies as I neared the celebration of finally going home. I had never been away from home for so long in my entire life. The thought of the comfort of my own soft bed with a crunchy duvet, after these horrible plastic mattresses and thin sheets, seemed like heaven. My doggies wagging their tails and having cuddles with me. Gosh, I felt like a child knowing that Christmas was getting close. I prayed that these last days would pass quickly.

In five days' time, Martin was coming for one more visit before discharge; we were to stay in the OT flat which was an adapted ground floor flat designed to give patients a chance to try normal life with their disability: a kind of stepping stone to the outside world. Some patients who lived closer would go home at weekends and then return to the unit; I think I would have found this quite distressing though, to see my dogs and my home only to be pulled back to the unit again.

I was quite excited at the prospect of our "mini-break" together and had quite a giggle with Karen asking if I should request that Martin bring me some sexy underwear for the night! Well, the dampers were soon put on when I saw the flat. It had its own front door, symbolising some level of independence but ironically there was another locked door within the flat that backed directly onto the OT suite. The flat was cold and stark, with no escaping the feeling that you were still in a hospital. Minimal furniture, emergency phones and cords everywhere, two single hospital beds with the familiar blue mattresses in the bedroom. I giggled, imagining Martin's face when he saw it, but knowing that we would still make the best of it.

Now a lot can happen in five days. Each day I continued to go to physio, with an increasing pressure to beat Shirley. She was walking without holding the bars now, and so I insisted on doing the same. I looked like a puppet without strings as I toddled forwards with my arms in front of me, trying to keep my balance. It was scary but I had the security of the bars on either side of me.

The next day I progressed to crutches and managed to walk about twenty steps around the physio room with Lisa following behind me with the wheelchair. It felt amazing. Martin was being sent updates by video and I loved how proud he was of me. There were dozens of comments from people cheering me on on Facebook too.

I was now allowed to have the Zimmer frame up in my room, which meant I could practise more steps. I would walk from my bed to the bathroom, and sometimes venture out to the nurses' station, always a little nervous and scared to go too far in case I needed to sit down. I would often stop off in Danny's room to sit down, feeling a little guilty as he was often in bed; but his face would light up, praising me for my progress, cheering me on.

Shirley and I would catch up daily in the dining room for lunch and compare notes on how we were doing. We were having a game of Connect 4 after our meal one day, when I noticed Danny was in the library with his little boy and an elderly couple. I couldn't concentrate on the game as I was mesmerised watching his little boy who was the most adorable little toddler. He was playing with the open and close button on the doors and successfully managed to open them giving me the pleasure of meeting him when he came out to see what Shirley and I were doing. He had the biggest brown eyes, perfect skin and that cute chubbiness that toddlers have. His gran came to rescue him from us and return him to his dad and the doors closed.

The next time the doors opened again, it was for their departure as they all waved goodbye to Danny. Then they were gone, and the doors closed. Danny was left in the library on his own. His back was facing me and Shirley, but I could sense he was upset. This was confirmed when I saw his grief-stricken shoulders heave up and down as he sobbed. I told Shirley I didn't know how long I would be, and I wheeled into the library at full speed to pull up beside him and put my arms around him.

'He was so scared of me in the wheelchair,' Danny sobbed.

I reassured him that this was only his first visit, that he would soon get used to it on future visits and how young children adapt so quickly. I sat and comforted him as much as I could, but my heart wanted to break. I literally could feel his pain as it brought back some very painful memories of my own.

I went to visit Danny in his room later that evening and was pleased to see his spirits had lifted courtesy of a visit from his friends. As we chatted, something happened that I had no idea was coming. I was surprised to find myself sharing with Danny just how my accident had happened. I guess I felt safe with him, perhaps because he had shared how he had suffered some mental health issues, or maybe due to the connection I felt with how he missed his son. We were talking about our injuries and our time in the early stages of recovery when it just spilled out of my mouth.

'I had a psychotic episode which led to me falling off a roof.'

Wow. I had said it. I had found my sentence.

'Christ, Nikki, that sucks,' he said. I realised that my biggest worry had been that people may think I had somehow caused my injury. That I was to blame and had been selfish in some way, perhaps deserving of my injury as a punishment. That I wasn't as "worthy" of being here in this hospital being helped with my recovery like them. Danny's reaction confirmed this was *not* the case and I certainly had no regrets sharing with him what had happened. It was a major breakthrough for me to have said it out loud and this was the beginning of me starting to find my voice. It had sounded a bit surreal though, almost as if it had happened to someone other than me!

I was always so relieved to get into my bed somewhere around 7.00 p.m. The exhaustion was like nothing I have ever experienced in my life. Sometimes I would have tears pouring down my face with sheer relief. Sadly, this exhaustion didn't bring about satisfying sleep; it was always very disturbed and I had not slept more than a consecutive two to three hours since this had all started. The nightly log rolls may have been the catalyst, but they had stopped now, since I was no longer at risk of bed sores. But I found it difficult to get comfortable, and my body would keep waking me up to either try and move or because I needed to shuffle my way to the toilet. The hospital gave me numerous meds to help; sleeping pills, tranquilisers, painkillers… but nothing worked, so I learnt to get by with minimal sleep. Perhaps my body was waiting to get home to my own bed.

The next day, Lisa took me to a quiet corridor to practise climbing stairs. We had managed two to three steps up to this point, but as my stairs at home were quite steep, we needed a bigger challenge. We had to wait as Shirley was in the stairwell in front of us, practising with her therapist. We smiled and said hello.

'How many sets did you do, Shirley?' asked Lisa as we swapped places

'Up and down twice today,' came the reply. Very clever, Lisa; she knew I would want to do three.

Martin was suitably impressed to discover I could now walk with two sticks when he arrived. I was still fully dependent on the wheelchair, but I could walk anywhere from ten to twenty steps before needing to sit down. I was constantly astounded at just how much was involved in learning to walk again. As well as building up strength in core muscles, I had to focus on not letting my left foot drag, ensuring I felt well balanced before stepping onto the other foot. The fear of falling was definitely greater than it must be for a toddler – well, it's further to fall for a start!

We decided to have a takeaway on our first night in the flat and it was somewhat surreal sitting on a sofa watching TV, pretending to be in a normal setting. I looked around the flat, picturing The Sims (a life simulation video game) that my girls used to play, giving the place some carpet, coloured walls, and checked curtains in my mind. A few pictures on the walls too, maybe.

There was no sneaking into each other's beds for a cuddle that night. Martin had made it quite clear he would want the okay from my consultant before any hanky panky could take place. He was scared I may be a little fragile; that he may cause me damage in some way. I would have my own list of questions for the consultant too, I decided, plus, I was ready to see the X-ray of my spine now.

The following morning, I asked Martin to take a photo of the scar on my back before getting ready for my hydro swimming session. This was a big step for me and I braced myself as I looked at the picture. Wow, it was about eight inches long and went all the way up to my bra strap from my knicker line. It was so neat though, kind of like a train track. My first war wound on my body! I certainly wouldn't want to try to cover it up with a tattoo like some people do, but maybe my backless dress days were over.

Martin was allowed at the poolside. I was nervous about trying to swim; the wimp in me was scared it would hurt my back now I had this piece of "Meccano" in there. I feared the intricate metalwork could possibly break if I moved awkwardly. I went from the wheelchair directly into the pool with the guidance of a metal bannister and ramp. I wasn't given any floats or swimming aids, so was relieved my feet could feel the bottom. I took a deep breath and bravely let my feet off the floor and plunged forward. I *was* able to swim, but my body couldn't move as it did before. My leg movements were small, and my arms took on most of the work almost as if to protect the lower back. Breaststroke was more uncomfortable than front crawl since it arched my back at an awkward angle; I took a few strokes but soon stopped to just float around. Overall, it was pleasant, but not quite the spectacular experience I had thought it would be. However, I imagine for someone fully paralysed it would be more of a cathartic experience.

Later that day we had an appointment with Sherlock and Dr Watson (the two psychiatrists). Martin took control from the start which I happily let him do. The last thing I wanted was another tiring interrogation like before, and I felt somewhat guarded. Having recapped what I had said before, we were both asked about the lead up to the event of falling from the roof. They, like most people, had assumed that I had jumped so I corrected them.

'It was more a case of throwing myself backwards,' I said, finding myself having to explain further. It was difficult trying to describe the psychosis, and I hated hearing just how crazy I sounded as I recounted all the sordid details.

The appointment ended successfully after about thirty minutes and I was told that someone from Mental Health would make contact with me once I was home to come and discuss my medication and any further counselling should I need it. They would send a copy of my report to my home address. Great, I would look forward to that! One thing that was clear to see, was that these two "detectives" were confused by how well my recovery was going. I imagined they probably presumed someone with a history of mental health issues of *any* kind, let alone "stress-induced" psychosis, would struggle with the stress of my situation— a broken back and now being in a wheelchair faced with a permanent disability. But here I was, thriving, happy, stronger than ever.

She will rise. With a spine of steel and a roar like thunder, she will rise. (Nicole Lyons)

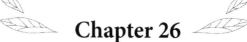

Chapter 26

Final Goodbyes

I don't think I could fully believe that I was finally going home the next day. It was like the Osborne ward had become my home, and some people may find this weird but I kind of liked it! I was feeling like a big fish in a small pond. I felt safe, with nurses all around me if I needed them.

I tried to picture myself at home and the immediate thing I worried about was the dogs knocking me off my sticks. Mabel is a very boisterous Labrador so she would have to learn quickly to be cautious around me. Chester probably wouldn't be such a problem; he was older and a bit slower these days.

Preparations had been taking place at home for my return. OT had been to visit our house and assess what aids were needed. I was having a handle fixed in our ensuite shower along with a seat apparently, the downstairs bathroom would have a bath seat and they would supply me with a perching stool in the kitchen, to rest on when preparing food. This was an area Martin and I had nearly come to blows with on our second night in the flat: he had tried to take over *all* the preparation of our meal right down to boiling the kettle. This frustrated the hell out of me, and I had forcefully insisted that he let me take part since I did not want to be pandered to like this at home. I wanted encouragement to find some independence to do the things that I could, otherwise I would feel useless. Yes, it took me a long time to shuffle around the kitchen, holding on to the work surface with both hands and walking sideways in a crab-like fashion. Yes, I had struggled to find a way to shut the fridge door whilst holding a pint of milk, but I needed to start practising finding solutions to the new dilemmas my body was presented with to get better. Oh, and to think how I scorned the prospect of OT in the early days!

Martin had installed two bannisters to help me with our stairs. OT had told me to plan my day carefully, ensuring that everything I needed was downstairs so that I didn't tire myself by climbing them during the day. I was thankful that the doors in our cottage wouldn't have to be widened since I wouldn't be using the wheelchair inside. The plan was to manage getting around purely with my walking sticks or holding on to furniture. A wheelchair had still been ordered for me though since I would need to use it when we went out. I was surprised therefore to hear that physio were reluctant to organise a wheelchair for Shirley.

'She's walking better than you, Nikki, totally different injury,' Martin said

'Er, no, she is not, she's not even using her Zimmer frame to walk around the ward yet, she relies on her wheelchair more than I do,' I argued, my nose well and truly out of joint.

I looked at the photos that Martin had sent me of the

home adjustments. The only picture missing was of our new front door, which he was keeping as a surprise; a stable door enabling me to open the top part to receive deliveries and prevent the dogs from pushing past me and causing havoc. The photo of the bannisters showed how the hallway had been freshly painted in "Swansdown" and I smiled, feeling somewhat like royalty having all this effort being made for my homecoming.

OT had warned me that my friends and family would need to learn to give me space, as if I had an invisible bubble around me, since my balance still wasn't good, and I could easily be knocked over. On a positive though, they said how I would carry on improving with my recovery, probably doubling in speed due to doing a lot more for myself and not using the wheelchair as much.

Shirley and I had our final lunchtime catch up; we swapped details and I knew that I was going to miss her and our daily chats. Her discharge date had been set for mid-October, two weeks after mine; possibly while arrangements were being put in place but also because she still needed a little more confidence. Did it feel good knowing I had beaten her to the finish line? Not particularly, not anymore. She had become my confidante, my partner in crime. We had found solace in comparing notes, sharing fears about our future, using each other as a sounding board. I am truly indebted to how she (unknowingly) spurred me on to aim high, to take those extra steps, to push that little bit harder. That very morning, I had tried walking without any aids, purely because I had seen Shirley doing exactly that...

Now, walking with no sticks or frame is like having the stabilisers taken off your bike, freewheeling, with the intense fear of falling over. With two physios on either side and ready to catch me, I took a leap of faith and stepped out, focusing on the wall ahead of me. It took great courage to put one foot in front of the other; I managed around eight steps before grabbing their arms for support.

Next, I had to take a series of tests (it felt like a mini exam) for physio to assess my improvement during my time on the ward. I passed with flying colours, nearly all items on the checklist being ticked; only the balance on my left side let me down a little. An item missing from the checklist, and another big win for me, was getting my socks on that morning: I had finally won the battle after getting dressed, feeling smug as a bug at not having to call a nurse to assist me; it told me I was ready to leave.

It was my final afternoon, and I was practising walking with two sticks up to the nurses' station and back to my room, only about ten metres or so, but it was my last chance to practise with the safety of having nurses in the vicinity. As I passed, Danny called out, 'Look at you!'

I tentatively walked into his room and plonked myself on a chair next to him. He was grinning from ear to ear, amazed with my progress. Now I cannot emphasise enough how guilty you can feel as an SCI "walker", and I first became aware of this at Sheffield. It could so easily have been me in Danny's position, feeling nothing below the waist, totally unable to experience the journey to walking again. It seemed so unfair, but then again everything is relative, isn't it? Danny was probably grateful on some level that he wasn't in the high dependency ward that I had passed. He was able to sit up in bed and play on his PlayStation, which by comparison was a giant step; he also had his ground-breaking moments.

I talked to him about my minions, telling him how much visualisation I had done and encouraging him to do the same. He didn't look perturbed by my "minion mania" and was suitably impressed when I told him how I had got my bowels and bladder back. We discussed how there were cases of complete injuries like his, with patients getting back sensation and even walking, years after their injury. We both decided he would be one of these "miraculous" cases in the future! I told him I felt bad showing off, coming in on my sticks when he was still unable to do a lift and shift.

'Don't be daft, darling. I'm proud of you. You're incredible and don't you forget it.'

He really was the kindest, sweetest human being. My heart melted as he told me his hopes for the future: all he wanted was to be able to have days out with his boy without struggling in his wheelchair, to have enough strength in his arms to do normal things such as going to the zoo. I reassured him that there was always the option of a motorised wheelchair and to believe, one way or another, that it would happen.

We swapped numbers and I made him promise to keep in touch as I wanted updates. I wanted to know how each stage of his recovery went and when he finally got out of this hospital. He may have been young enough to be my son, but somehow, I knew that we would be friends; I could feel it in my water.

My final afternoon in Sheffield is one I will never forget. I thought I had died and gone to wheelchair heaven. I went down to the sports hall for a "wheelchair skills" class to discover that the table tennis tables had been set out. For most of my childhood, we had a table tennis table and for many years my dad used to challenge me to beat him. He would give himself a handicap to give me a better chance, such as playing with his left hand or giving me ten points advantage, always taunting me to get better and better until one day I finally beat him fair and square. Well, my handicap was being in a wheelchair today, and I would have loved to have challenged him.

I had to tell myself to calm down more than once; this was just a little bit of fun, Nikki, it was not about winning. I worked at keeping my patience levels in check whilst playing against people who could barely get the ball over the net. I was itching to have a good rally, a proper game, and then someone heard my prayers. One of the helpers had been watching me and challenged me to a game. He sat in a chair to make it even.

The ball pinged backwards and forwards with the sports hall coming to a standstill as everyone stopped to watch. I started doing little smashes with my forehand, my previous experience all coming back to me, and then, before I knew it, we were at a tiebreak and my excitement reached fever pitch. With match point in my favour, my opponent dropped the ball just over the net which I knew I would never reach from my wheelchair, so I stood up… and holding on to the table I leant forwards and hit the ball. Everyone's faces were hilarious. They obviously didn't know that I wasn't paralysed and could do this. Game to Rodwell.

Table tennis party over, and I was like an over-excited child. I didn't want it to end. I even questioned if I had rushed a little too fast with my goal to get home as it was so much fun here. I revealed how I felt as I chatted with Karen.

'It's perfectly normal, I told you when you arrived that you would feel sad about leaving, some people do,' she said. 'But you need to go home and get back to your life, to discover your "new normal".' A phrase I would be reminded of, often.

Oh, I would miss her and our chats. She was so down to earth and, like me, the child within was always looking for a way to escape and have a giggle. She was a little bit naughty with a dash of feistiness and I knew that in another world, she was someone that would make an amazing friend. Of course, nurses and patients are not allowed to develop friendships and I knew this, but she would stay fondly imprinted in my heart and I hoped our paths may cross again one day, perhaps if I ever came back for an appointment. She came back one more time, to say her final goodbye before going off shift that evening. I presented her with a little Tropic gift and as she hugged me; she said she was going to miss me too, and I'm sure I saw a tear in her eye.

As I lay in bed, I was so excited about the thought of seeing my dogs again, that I needed something to distract me, so I decided to write my first blog. I had managed to set up a site on my MacBook and wanted a way to talk about my experience. I had decided that I would share my journey, and, when I felt brave enough, tell people how it had happened. First, though, I had an idea in my head that I was going to find the courage to disclose it to my Tropic friends at our next team meeting. Having told Danny, I now pictured myself standing at the front of our meeting and telling the ladies in my team how mental health had dealt me this trick hand and led me to falling off that roof.

If people judged me then they weren't friends, I was coming to terms with this now. I needed to get over my fear that people would see me as the knife-wielding maniac in the Psycho films and believe that they would judge me on what was in front of them, the strong, determined, kind, and well-balanced person that I am. I believe we all need to see the good in people, and if we don't understand something, then we need to better educate ourselves. Mental health does not define a person and my psychosis would not define me.

Chapter 27

The Homecoming

I barely slept a wink that last night, too excited at the prospect of seeing my dogs and being back in the comfort of my own home. Martin arrived at 9.00 a.m. with bags and cases to pack up my room whilst I sat and watched, telling him all about the table tennis session. It was strange watching my "home", with all its memories, being packed up into bags and cases; the end of a chapter, the end of my *new* education, although I suspected I would still have a lot to learn once back in the real world.

'Sounds like you don't want to come home,' he laughed.

'All good things come to an end,' I replied. 'Nothing's permanent, everything's temporary.'

We both went to my final appointment with the consultant who showed me the X-ray of my fractured vertebrae; it took my breath away. The perfect row of vertebrae sat aligned from my neck downwards until T12, which was blitzed into pieces with a shard leaning into the dark canal that was my spinal cord. It struck me how strange it was that none of the other vertebrae had been damaged, just the one, like a box of crystal glasses that had been dropped from a great height but only one had shattered. The next photo showed the repair, with little screws and bolts being greatly magnified in the X-ray. I took photos with my iPhone to add to the photo Martin had taken of the scar on my back; these were my tablets of stone reminding me that inside that scar, little titanium rods were holding my spine together. That my back wasn't the same anymore… it was fragile.

Then came the awkward topic of sex, Martin expressing his concern that he may hurt me, wanting to know just how fragile I was.

'You're not *that* big, darling,' I laughed, trying to cover up my embarrassment. We were told that it would be fine and informed how occasionally, sexual sensation returned to some patients meaning it may even be enjoyable. Pah! Little did they know; I had already checked this out the other night and actually, I would say sensation was heightened in that department. No, all was okay apart from one slightly concerning thing— a few seconds before orgasm occurred, my feet went into a spasm and all my toes curled up. I wasn't about to ask if this was normal, but it certainly gave a whole new meaning to having a "toe-curling" experience! Yet again I was very lucky; sexual sensation had resumed, no permanent damage there.

After my final physio session, where I practised walking in the corridor with Martin following behind me, I made my final goodbyes as we collected my bags. Then after three arduous months of recuperation, I finally walked out of Sheffield Northern General on 4 October just four days over my goal which everyone had laughed at. I had the wheelchair right behind me, but I WALKED out to the car waiting outside, with the aid of two walking sticks.

Whilst I had aimed for the moon and narrowly missed, I had certainly landed in the stars— lucky stars that I would be thanking for some time to come.

After an uneventful journey back to Norfolk, we finally pulled up on the gravel driveway and my emotions took over. I looked across the fence at our beautiful cottage with the roses around the door and the perfectly-sized front garden. I couldn't help but cry and I bit my lip to stop it from shaking, knowing who was waiting inside for me. I had been dreaming of this moment for so long.

Martin went in ahead of me to put Mabel and Chester in the kitchen, giving me a safe pathway to sit myself down in the lounge before greeting them. I briefly noticed the new front door but was more taken aback with the silver-ribboned banner saying, "Welcome Home", which kept the tears streaming down my face. It was hard to absorb; there were balloons and "Welcome Home" banners all around the lounge and a celebratory cake on the table. Our cleaner, Jaz, had done all this for me. She was the sweetest girl.

'Welcome home, Screwfix,' Martin said. This was to be his new term of endearment for me!

Once I was safely sitting on the sofa, the dogs were let in. They were so excited, tails wagging, excited that their dad was back home to them, sniffing around the cake on the table, but then they clocked there was a guest. Rushing over, Mabel sniffed me and cowered away initially, which really upset me. She didn't seem to recognise me.

'What's up with her?'

'Give her time, she can smell hospitals.'

I patted the sofa next to me to signal for them to jump up and join me since the rules had been relaxed in my absence and they were now allowed to do this! Chester bounced up; he knew who I was immediately and didn't hesitate to come for cuddles. Mabel cautiously followed him, getting up beside me and then, all of a sudden, the penny dropped. She remembered who I was and started climbing all over me licking and sniffing and whimpering excitedly, re-uniting with her mummy.

I was home at last, where my heart belonged.

EPILOGUE

We will all face adversities of one kind or another, that is guaranteed, and I'm sure I still have plenty more to come. But for now, I embrace the lessons, the "gift" that this particular experience has given me. I appreciate the small everyday things that I once took for granted, sitting on the toilet in my ensuite and taking in the view across the fields, being out in nature with my dogs, standing and washing my hair in the shower, or putting my socks on!

As for my mental state, well, I can honestly say that writing this memoir has been incredibly healing. It has taught me to confront the stigma of mental health and address the deep and hidden psychoses that I hadn't even realised I had been avoiding; making the invisible become visible. The process of writing has slowly peeled back many layers of guilt and embarrassment, revealing the true and authentic version of me. Being open and honest has finally legitimised the traumatic episodes that have happened in my past, some of which ended in admission to psychiatric hospital. It has allowed me to finally heal for those times as well as addressing them with my daughters too.

The realisation that I was a victim of mental health stigma has empowered me to break its chains, and, I believe, put that dark beast called psychosis to rest once and for all; you have to face your biggest fears to take away their power. You have to let go of fear of judgement from others to be true to yourself and find freedom.

I used to hide behind a veil of denial whereas now I proudly say, 'Mental health broke my back, but it didn't break me.'

Note

If you or anybody you know suffers or have suffered with mental health issues, please know you are not alone and that it's okay to not be okay. Please be brave and seek support and/or medical advice. Please know that my message is one of hope and finding light in the darkness.

Can You Help?

Thank You For Reading My Book!

I really appreciate all of your feedback, and I love hearing what you have to say. If you are able to, please leave me an honest review on Amazon letting me know what you thought of the book – it would mean the world to me as a new author. Or you can just leave a star rating. You might not think your opinion matters, but I can assure you it does. It helps the book to gain visibility and helps other readers to decide whether to purchase it, so if you could take a minute or two it would be much appreciated. If you have a paperback in your hand and think 'this request doesn't include me', please think again. It doesn't matter how or where you bought your paperback, Amazon, Goodreads and BookBub will still accept a review from you.

Thank you

Nikki

Acknowledgments

First and foremost to my beloved husband Martin Rodwell for standing by me in sickness and in health and never losing faith that I would come through. Also, for tirelessly listening to me read chapters of this book and cheering me on when I doubted myself. And, of course, for making me laugh, every day.

To my daughters— my youngest Angel for her love and protection during the crisis and for highlighting to me the difficulties of such a trauma from her perspective.
To my middle daughter for her love and support during the writing of my book.
To my eldest for being brave and strong and warming my heart by calling me 'Mummy Bear'.

To my dear friend Ulli Gale for your numerous bedside visits. To Kat Tindall for my funky socks and help with my physio exercises, also for being my verbal punchbag with expletive competitions! To Helen Colebrooke for coming to cut my fringe before I went to Sheffield. To Dan Rayner and Andrea Wilson for your visits and making me laugh. To Jenny Tribe for wonderful massage and soul nourishment. To all the other friends, neighbours, and team members who popped in to see me even if I was asleep.

To my Tropic colleagues for the visits you made to see me in hospital plus the support when I whinged in the chat groups; you were a lifeline at times. For the weird and wonderful gifts you sent me and of course to the special ladies who came to shave my legs! A special mention also to the ladies who helped me back to my hotel room at the leaders' event!

To all the amazing NHS staff for what they do. At the N&N my particular thanks to the 'singing' nurse for her hugs and love. Also, to the spinal surgeons who performed my operation. At Sheffield Spinal Unit, a big thanks to everyone for seeing me through 'big school'. A special mention to one lady in particular for helping me pull up my 'big girl pants'.

Danny Byrne and Shirley Rees for being such amazing fellow SCI patients and now friends.

To the Back Up Trust Charity – for amazing support and teaching me about SCI.

Book Support – Alison Williams for being such a sensitive and supportive editor whilst tactfully helping me to improve my writing and guiding me with this book. I could not have done it without her.

Julia Gibbs for introducing me to the Twitter writing world and answering numerous questions along the way. Also for being a fabulous friend!

Cutting Edge – book design

Joe Ringer – logo design

Self-Publishing School— for setting me off on this journey.

Mary Matthews of Three Shires Publishing – for publishing/marketing advice and calming my nerves!

To the many authors and writers who have given support and advice and much needed blog posts on writing and self-publishing.

Free exclusive content:

Thank you so much for sharing my journey by reading 'Catch Me if I Fall'. I love to interact with my readers and would like to continue sharing my journey with you via my newsletter. If you sign up to that here **https:// nikkirodwell.co.uk/book-readers**/, I will send you my free gift of the photo journey of my book, only available to my subscribers, for free.

Printed in Great Britain
by Amazon